ESCAPE

The Magix Series
Book Two

Written by
P RYALL

Escape

Copyright © P Ryall

Escape, The Magix Series: Book Two

First published 2022

Email: p.ryall13@gmail.com

ISBN:

eBook: 978-1-923493-75-9
Paperback: 978-1-923493-76-6
Hardcover: 978-1-923493-77-3

All rights reserved. Without limiting the rights under copyright reserved above, no part of this publication may be reproduced, stored in or introduced into a database and retrieval system or transmitted in any form or any means (electronic, mechanical, photocopying, recording or otherwise) without the prior written permission of both the owner of copyright and the above publishers.

This book is copyright. Apart from any fair dealing for the purposes of private study, research, criticism or review permitted under the *Copyright Act 1968*, no part may be stored or reproduced by any process without prior written permission. Enquiries should be made to the publisher

This is a work of fiction. Names, characters, places and incidents are the produce of the author s imagination or used factitiously. Any resemblance to the actual events, locales, or persons, living or dead, is entirely coincidental.

P Ryall

This book is dedicated to my parents, without whom I would never have been courageous enough to chase my dreams.

My youngest daughter, for the constant creative spirit you share and your brave sense of self, you teach me every day how to be a better and more authentic person. I adore you.

Escape

Acknowledgements

P Ryall

Table of Contents

Acknowledgements iv
Chapter 1 1
Chapter 2 12
Chapter 3 24
Chapter 4 39
Chapter 5 51
Chapter 6 59
Chapter 7 64
Chapter 8 73
Chapter 9 80
Chapter 10 89
Chapter 11 99
Chapter 12 115
Chapter 13 123
Chapter 14 133
Chapter 15 148
Chapter 16 166
Chapter 17 185
About the Author 199

Chapter 1

Lilah stirred. Her eyes were heavy. The buzzing in her head quickly escalated to a pounding sensation. She remembered her name now—but her memories were fuzzy and out of order. There were a lot of blanks, things she didn't remember at all. How long had she been unconscious? Who, or what, had attacked her? Was she in the A.S.U or had she been taken to another hospital? Her mother wasn't here, otherwise she would've been fussing about. If she opened her eyes, she would surely get these answers, but she wasn't sure she wanted to know. Not yet.

Finally, she grudgingly let her eyes utter open a fraction…and screamed. A face was less than two inches from hers.

Peter startled awake and blinked at her with wide, confused eyes.

"Sorry, I didn't realise you were there," she mumbled, going bright red and covering her mouth with her hands.

"Christ, I thought someone was trying to do you in again," he rasped, still looking around. "Dammit. That scared the life out of me." His breathing evened out then he sighed and sat up. "Sorry, guess I scared you first." He grinned.

Lilah smacked his arm lightly and stuck out her tongue then giggled.

Escape

The doors at the far end of the wing opened, and three people came striding in, weapons at the ready. "What's happened?" Bryant demanded as he scanned every inch of the room, looking for an enemy.

"No, no, it's all right." Lilah was blushing so much now she was almost glowing. "I'm so sorry. I was startled when I woke up. Honestly, it's just a misunderstanding" Blinking rapidly, she tried to keep tears at bay as her embarrassment grew. She couldn't look at her would-be protectors, so she focused on her blanket, twisting the ends of her hair anxiously.

Peter sighed. "Actually, I was the reason she screamed. I fell asleep and ended up sharing a pillow with her." He grimaced, but his voice was even.

She didn't know what she'd expected, really, but thunderous laughter wasn't it. Morti ed, she wanted to dig a hole and hide in it for all eternity. When Bryant's chortles finally quietened, she dared a peek. Why weren't the other Taylors with him? The two men flanking him were unmistakably human, with full combat gear, and rearms, and small earpieces lodged in their ears. One smiled sheepishly at her when he saw her looking, but the other was too absorbed in whatever Bryant and Peter were talking about now.

"She broke the restraints. We didn't anticipate how strong she would be here. I have added extra security and we are keeping her wings clamped—at least until we can figure out who she is. I was thinking that if we put the other one with her, well, close to her cell anyway, we could maybe catch her name. Clearly, she's a queen, though." Bryant shrugged absently.

Peter considered him thoughtfully. "I doubt it will be a good idea, and honestly, having them near each other will get

Matt really pissed—he just found them, and they're alive. He won't want to chance it."

Lilah sat there, stunned into silence. There was plenty she wanted to say, but not right now. *Matt*. Her dad was here. It was only just dawning on her now that her family, her only blood relatives apart from her brother, were so close…yet she felt no desire to see them. It was too soon. Then it hit her, her mother—her adopted one—was an Aggaron. Lilah worked hard to keep her emotions controlled. She didn't want to scare anyone—or make them laugh. She couldn't tell anyone about her mother either. If it got out that even one Aggaron had survived and was here… She shuddered. The Huntowra were ruthless, and they wouldn't stop at killing the Aggaron.

Peter had stopped speaking mid-sentence and came to her side. "Hey. It's going to be okay, you know? We won't let them get anywhere near you. Not again." He reached out to soothe her.

She wasn't scared of the Huntowra prisoners, but his gentle tone made her smile softly anyway. He sighed and glanced at the others. They bowed slightly and turned, and it took her a minute to realise they'd bowed to her. It was weird, but she supposed if she'd grown up in her home, it would've been perfectly normal. She was tired again but didn't want to sleep. Peter was looking at her like he was trying to figure out what she was thinking. Did he think she was crazy?

"No, I don't think that at all," he said gruffly.

She jumped. He'd answered her thought. How did he do that?

Escape

"You have a telepathic ability, but apparently you haven't remembered that yet." He sounded exhausted. Had he slept at all?

He yawned and moved to the cot next to hers. She wanted him to stay with her, but that would be selfish. He was tired and needed sleep. She just lay there and watched silently while he dozed off. When he was soundly sleeping, she let her thoughts wander again. She needed to be careful not to let her thoughts be heard, but she honestly wasn't sure how to stop herself from doing whatever it was that made her do it.

* * *

Peter had been watching over Lilah, but his own exhaustion took hold of him. He needed rest, and lots of it. But every time he closed his eyes, he saw it all again. The sight of her, frozen on the stairs, surrounded by Starling Trumpets. Her eyes boring into him. A flash of something and then… He cringed. And then…and then she was lying there, so very still, like a sleeping angel. His heart had pounded in his chest so hard it was a wonder it hadn't popped right out. In that moment, he'd known he had to save her, that he was the only one who could. There wasn't even a choice, and he'd acted without any thought whatsoever for his own wellbeing.

He'd glimpsed his brother, Ethan, looking at her helplessly, twitching. Why hadn't he done anything to help her? Ethan's had always been close to Lilah, almost as close as he was. That his brother loved her as fiercely as he did was odd yet comforting. It hadn't even shocked him when his brother had offered his hand. Sure, he'd been relieved that the bonds hadn't formed, but that was purely because of how he felt. It was selfish to want to keep her for himself, but if the bonds *had* formed, he would've been ecstatic for his brother. It was their way. Talgra loved intensely, but since coming to Earth, he'd realised that some of their customs were...kind of weird when it came to bonding.

As he slept, his mind raced, and he heard some of Lilah's thoughts as well, though they were muted from his exhaustion and her attempts to stop them from penetrating his mind. He wanted to smile or say something to her about it, but he didn't. Instead, he let the thoughts and images wash over him, enjoying not having peace. After all these years of deafening silence, this was bliss. He slowly drifted off to her thoughts. The last he remembered was a flash of a smiling woman, reaching out as though to hug him. A memory, he supposed. She seemed...familiar, somehow. His mind flew then, and he was asleep before he could make any sense of what he'd seen.

Lilah lay there with her eyes closed, hoping to sleep again, but her tiredness wasn't physical. A soft creak of the doors told her someone was there, and the light padding of steps said whoever it was wasn't in a hurry. She wondered who it could be but was too nervous to check. With a sigh, the visitor sat down but didn't speak. After a while, she nodded off again. She didn't know how long she slept for, but she woke to a hushed conversation.

"How has she been? She always seems to be asleep when I'm here. Is that normal?" It was her father. He sounded stressed and tired. They were all on edge, though.

"I really can't say, Matt. She suffered an extreme trauma after significant drainage of her magix. The power bands had been embedded into her body and were killing her. Honestly, I don't know that she *will* fully recover. Whatever we do, it might

Escape

not be enough for her body to heal from this level of damage. I've never seen anyone with this number of injuries, not even Frank from Helios, and we both know how scrappy he was." Evaliah sighed, sounding frustrated.

She opened her eyes a fraction and looked across, sure that her father and Eva were caught up in talking. Peter was staring at her, also lying there quietly. His lip twitched, and he nodded a little.

"Shh." It was a mental hush; he didn't want them to know they were being overheard.

"Can you hear me?" she thought.

He nodded again.

"Why can't we let them know we're awake? They aren't saying anything important. Not really."

He looked straight ahead for a moment. *"Because Matt's been in a war meeting. They're making travel arrangements to start moving us all back to Meakra soon. We are keeping this place as a secondary base, though, so we'll travel between them as needed."*

Lilah's jolted, and her eyes flew open.

Matt and Eva rushed to her side.

"Lilah, honey, can you hear me?" Evaliah felt Lilah's forehead and took her pulse. "It's okay. You're safe, you had us all worried there. We didn't know how long you would sleep for." She smiled so sweetly that Lilah relaxed.

She didn't respond though; she simply didn't feel up to talking yet.

"Lilah?" It was her dad, and though he only said her name, she knew he was asking if she was okay, if she needed anything or was in any pain.

Lilah grabbed his hand, and he held it gently between both of his. She gave him a tiny smile, blinking slowly. "I'm 'kay," she murmured softly. Then she faked a yawn, hoping they would let her rest. She wasn't tired now, but she did want to talk to Peter. The idea of him going back to Meakra had her worried. She would miss him if he left.

Instead of leaving, though, her dad sat on her bed and spoke softly. "Your brother didn't even say two words to me. He just left in a hurry. Now he's not answering my calls. I think he's in shock, but he checks in on you a lot. He should be coming by soon. I think."

"He can be funny like that. He's always had to be strong for Mama and me." She shrugged, not worried about Dae's reaction. He had been sad not to have a dad growing up, but he'd done his best to emulate Troy, the man who would've been his…their father. "Just give him space to process everything. He'll come to you when he's ready."

In truth, she didn't know if he would, she just didn't want to hurt their father's feelings. Neither of them knew what had happened to the rest of their biological family, apart from their mother, who'd died in their mama's arms. At this point in his life, Dae was happy and content being the man he hoped Troy would have been proud of. He took care of his family, he was kind, he cared for those who needed help and he didn't break women's hearts; well not on purpose anyway. On the occasions he had, he'd felt really awful about it and sulked for weeks.

Escape

Matt took a deep breath, clearly about to say something, when the doors opened again.

"Where is my son? He has hidden out here enough now. I demand you let me speak with him." Camilla was furious, and Lilah giggled nervously as Peter rolled his eyes.

Camilla stopped dead then rushed forward and wrapped her in a bear hug so tight she squeaked.

"Oops, sorry, my sweet. How are you? It's been hell without you here, and my son's being a total brat. We all missed you very much." She peppered Lilah's face with kisses and stroked her hair, much as her mother did. It was sweet and scary at the same time.

"I've missed you too, Milly," she squeaked, and the woman burst into tears.

"Oh, by the heavens above, I'm sorry. It's just given me so much hope for us all, having you here. Though my son's life might be in peril, naughty pup that he is."

She frowned at him darkly, but he just stared back innocently, not speaking. Lilah was reminded of a time when they were younger. Ethan had been playing pranks on everyone, and of course Peter got the blame for it. One of the downsides of being an identical twin, she supposed, but to her it was hilarious. All his brothers were mischief makers, and Peter was often the one who got into trouble for their mischief. Lilah felt a tightness in her lower throat, as though she wanted to cry. She knew more about his life than he did. She needed to keep it to herself, though, so she focused hard on his mother and how she was fussing over him now.

Peter tried to shove her hands away, like a small child would, and she smacked his hand then went back to tucking his blanket in around him. "I'm a grown up, ya know."

"Don't you take that tone with me. I am your mother. I gave you life. Be careful or I might just remove it as well." She glared at him harshly, and he reddened.

They only stopped staring at each other when Lilah giggled again, this time a hearty chortle and not her usual wispy one. Camilla spun round and relaxed, and Peter's eyes narrowed suspiciously, but he said nothing. He chewed his bottom lip and glanced down at his hands, folded in front of him.

"Sorry," Lilah gasped between fits of giggles.

"Lilah, it isn't appropriate for a crown princess to giggle like that. I know it's been a rough few days, but you are royalty. Please remember that," her father chided gently, though he had a very soft expression. She wasn't being told off, just reminded that it was expected of her to remain dignified.

"Pfft," she snorted. "I haven't been raised that way here, Da. I have a business to run, friends I swap clothes with...I even get into arguments sometimes. I was raised as a normal *mortal* child, so I'm not really worried about protocol." Though her words were soft, she gave her father a steely look that said clearly she wasn't going to be silenced.

At the rebuff, his shoulders slumped but then he raised his chin. "That may be so, but you *are* a royal, you *will* inherit my throne, and you *will* get judged by our people. Like it or not, this is who you *are*." He stood. "Forgive me, I have matters to attend to. I will come back this evening. Hopefully then, you'll have had adequate rest."

Escape

His words were kind and yet, he had a tone of authority she couldn't remember from when she was younger. This war had changed him, but anyone would be changed if they lost their whole family, she supposed. She nodded politely and watched as he retraced his steps to the door, and she felt a jolt of anxiety as it shut behind him.

"Wait, no, come back." She realised as soon as she thought it that Peter had heard her.

* * *

Peter heard her mental panic. She'd never been anxious as a child so hearing it in her voice worried him. But he kept trying to compare her now to who she'd been before, before the trauma and God knows how much violence and brutality. He doubted she would want anyone to know what she had suffered, and he didn't want to ask. Not right now.

His mother finally finished fussing over them. He suspected Lilah had been distracting her, and he was thankful for it. It seemed she knew he was feeling raw and not at all up to visitors today. He just wanted to spend time with Lilah, even if they were both sleeping or staring off into space. His mother left after doling out more stern warnings about his impending demise for what he'd done.

Peter glanced at Lilah as the doors swung closed again, but before he could speak, she flopped back into her pillow and sighed. *"She's really mad at you, huh?"*

"Are you gonna only talk in your head now? I'll look like I've gone insane, talking to myself and all. They're already looking at me with fear, you know?" He didn't elaborate, but she knew what he meant.

"Thank you. I know it was hard for you to show them so much of your true self. You've hidden it so well all these years, haven't you?" She propped her head on her arm and gave him a genuine smile.

"Yeah, well, it was that or have you die. Again. And I am not going through that again, Lilah. Even Ethan would agree. You're more important to us than hiding some powers, even if they mean I'm a freak of nature."

He'd always had worries about her best friend, his twin. He kept saying that she could easily replace him with Ethan, the 'funnier' brother, but she'd only ever wanted to be his friend. There was no need for Peter to feel so unsure. She didn't really know what to say, so she sat quietly and just enjoyed the moment.

Chapter 2

Ethan and Jess were in the Talgra's training room, sparring. She was determined and strong, so he felt safe enough not holding back when fighting her. They'd done this since Lilah was abducted. The emperor had wanted his other heirs to be trained so they, at least, could defend themselves. Emma was determined not to train with them, saying she would do her own, and her grandfather had eventually agreed, as long as she could show that she was learning, which she had.

Jess jabbed him hard in the ribs. He hadn't been paying attention, and she smirked when he grunted. "Don't get cocky, princess," he sneered. She hated being called that.

"Stuff it, you pompous brat. You think being from such an infamous bloodline will save you when the Huntowra come to kill us all? Get a clue. What were you daydreaming about anyway?"

"Lilah." He shrugged and reached for his water bottle.

"Oh, *perfect*," she snarled.

She was annoyed with him again. No surprise there. She was always annoyed or angry at him, but it wasn't a bad thing. He often didn't pay enough attention anyway. She wasn't angry that he was thinking of Lilah, though; she was never angry about her cousin. Everyone assumed she was, because she was a tough woman, but underneath that, she was a very nurturing person.

Ethan often wished he could offer her his hand, and she felt the same. It just hadn't happened…but while they both remained unattached, there was still hope. Of course, they could see each other romantically if they wanted to, there were no rules against that, but they wanted it to be more than a fling. And what if they fell in love and then another came along and was bonded to one of them? It was better this way.

"Listen, I have to go. Emma's finishing early, and we're checking out some new restaurant she found. Something about galaxies or stars or something, I think. Anyway, she seems excited, so…yeah." Jess grabbed her bag and towel, gave Ethan a longing look, and then turned away when she realised he'd stripped off his shirt.

He smiled in her direction, knowing she would be embarrassed by his 'nudeness,' as she called it. It made him feel smug that she was so affected by his body. "That sounds great. Have fun tonight. And say hi to Em. I'm off to annoy my idiot brother." He rolled his eyes.

"Which one?"

"The one who blew himself up the other day, of course." He shook his head like he was exasperated but folded his arms defensively across his chest. He was worried. It was natural, especially for twins.

She didn't say anything, just nodded in understanding.

Ethan had showered and paced the halls for over an hour before deciding to go see his brother. Truthfully, he was anxious about seeing Lilah again, though he didn't know why. She was his best friend from childhood; it seemed weird to feel self-conscious around her now. Of course, he hadn't offered his hand to her before. She'd already been taken in a much more

Escape

permanent way with the eternal bracelet, and so he'd always restrained himself, out of respect for his brother. But now he'd finally offered, and he was scared Peter would feel uncomfortable with him being near.

He finally gave up pacing and just went to see him. The doors were closed, indicating someone was resting, but he knew he would be allowed in. He quietly opened the doors, not looking up until they were secure behind him. When he did look, both Peter and Lilah were awake and sitting cross-legged on their beds, facing each other. They seemed to be having a staring contest of some kind while eating their meals, occasionally nodding or shrugging.

He'd seen them like this before. It had been funny to watch: Lilah in her berry tree and Peter on a makeshift swing, both silent, and yet they seemed to smile together, or laugh unexpectedly. Ethan hadn't told anyone; he assumed this was the bracelets at work or something. Maybe he'd been wrong to dismiss it so easily.

"Hey." He tried for casual, but they jumped apart guiltily and he couldn't help snorting. "Sorry, didn't mean to scare you guys. Figured I would come and hang out for a bit. Jess is getting some dinner with Emma. How much longer are you two stuck here for?" He grabbed an apple from Peter's tray and took a bite.

"Don't know. Actually, we were wondering that too. Eva is being extra careful, with Lilah's condition and all." Peter looked pointedly at her then at Ethan. "Took you long enough to come visit us. We were thinking you didn't like us anymore." There was a teasing light in Peter's eyes.

Ethan gave him a cocky, lopsided grin, and the weirdness vanished.

* * *

They had an enjoyable evening, just hanging out, chatting. Lilah was telling them all about life here on Earth, and her friends who'd spoiled her while she was so sick. Ethan and Peter wore identical expressions of interest and asked endless questions about this world. She barely had any answers for her own questions, but she didn't mind much. They were both happy.

Finally, Ethan left to get some sleep, and Eva finished her nightly rounds, which left Peter and Lilah alone for the night—with room dividers for modesty, or so Matt had said. He'd been so tired when he came back; the meetings he'd been in had gotten heated. Lilah felt sorry for upsetting him earlier that day, but she refused to be told to behave. Their conversation was nicer this time, but the stiff, formal way he spoke told her he was ready to just go and sleep.

He'd picked her some Kashiers, a flower native to their home, Meakra. They resembled tulips, though they were larger, with silvery-green leaves. These were a pale violet, but they came in every colour imaginable, and they smelled like jasmine and caramel. She loved Kashiers, and she wondered if they were imported and grown here or if they'd come straight from their home world. She didn't ask though; she was too busy smelling them. When she looked up to thank her father, he was looking at her with a soft expression.

"You look so much like your mother. I miss her dearly. It's such a huge blessing just to know that you and your brother are alive, and relatively healthy. I know I haven't been there in your lives, but I do hope that you will let me be a part of the future; whatever that looks like."

Escape

His sincerity made her gulp, swallowing a lump in her throat. "I'd like that," she said quietly. She wanted to get out of here, to see her mother and brother. There was a lot to discuss, and she felt homesick, for her Earth home.

Peter yawned. He'd been staying awake to keep her company, so she stretched out and settled in for the night.

* * *

She was dreaming again, only now she knew what the dream was. It was the day she'd been abducted and thrown to the Shrogan. She was racing to the ground, hordes of eyes looking up at her, more looking down from above. One of the Huntowra fell a few feet, and the others raced to catch him, before a portal opened, and they vanished. She flipped over again then, and saw tufts of hair, and the ground. Pain exploded in her, and a white light, tinged with green, surrounded her as she lost consciousness.

She woke up in a sort of cocoon. The moment she began to feel claustrophobic, the cocoon cracked open, and she stood up. The cocoon was her length, and there was a soft mist that somehow seemed alive in the bottom half. She looked around and saw a network of darkened caves that looked abandoned. Just then she heard a guttural growling, and before she could think about it, she was dashing for the cave, wanting to hide from whatever was making the sound.

When she got into the darkness, she felt a chill from behind her. She turned and saw the cave was more like a tube. Light was coming from somewhere far off in the distance. Curious, she started automatically down the tunnel. She wasn't as scared as she'd been outside, with the monsters growling, but she wished she was somewhere else, somewhere safe. There was something else, something important she should've been doing. Her mind fought to remember, but she couldn't get it to work right.

After a while of walking and thinking, she came out into a massive underground cavern. There were large rocks in all kinds of pretty colours everywhere. Some were bigger than trees, others were about her size. In the centre of the cavern was a lake so big she couldn't see the ends of it in any direction. The lake was dimly lit from the depths, but it was enough to see creatures swimming in the water. Strangely shaped, pale pink balls with lots of legs, or arms, were gently walking along the bottom of the edges. She reached out to touch one, but she scared it. The creature let out a bright blue cloud that faded to a gentle glow within minutes then vanished altogether.

She didn't try to touch any more of the creatures; instead, she walked around the walls of the cavern looking for more tunnels. She found a few twice as large as the one she'd just been in, and she was pleased to find a grove of fruit trees. The fruit was bitter but reminded her of something she'd tried once... Her mind went blank again. Nothing. Not even a hint of what she'd been thinking a moment ago. As she wandered, chewing on the fruit, she saw smaller animals here and there, but she wasn't scared of them.

The dream shifted again. She was outside now in the harsh desertscape, the brightness hurting her eyes. She was watching the cliff faces around her, looking for the screeches that had scared her on that first day here. Now, she'd been watching them from within the safety of the caves and she knew that the noises were their way of talking to each other. Not paying attention, she stumbled on a rock, and as she straightened, she saw it. A huge stairway, leading up into the

Escape

cliffs. It seemed to pull her toward it, and without really meaning to, she started climbing. After a long time, she reached the top and saw what looked like an old, ruined city. At the far end, there were large doors, and as she made her way across the floor to them, there was a rumble so big the whole world trembled.

* * *

Lilah woke in a sweat, a scream escaping her. Peter was already at her side, reaching for her. She shivered as the remnants of her memory faded, and she woke fully. She grabbed his arm and pulled him close, so he was hugging her. She was still shaking, and her forehead was dripping with cold sweat.

"Hey, what happened?" Peter asked her quietly.

"It was a dream. Just a dream," she replied, her voice barely a whisper. She didn't want to worry him. "It's ne. Just give me a minute, 'kay."

"Take as long as you need. I'm right here. You're safe now." He sat there quietly, holding her until the shivers subsided.

She felt embarrassed then, not wanting to seem weaker than she already was. Neither of them spoke again until the next morning, when he kept the conversation as casual as he could. She decided to follow his example, and half an hour after breakfast, Eva came in to tell them there was no point keeping them in the infirmary any longer. She also gave strict instructions to come back for check-ups and that if they had any side effects, any at all, they must return immediately. Nobody knew what side effects could come from being blown apart.

Lilah went pale at the thought, but Peter just shrugged in agreement. He gathered his clothes, and shoes, and the gifts from his family. Lilah didn't have much. The only ones who'd visited her were her brother and father. And Peter, of course, but as he was in the bed next to hers, it didn't really count.

She hummed to herself as she collected her costume and the Kashiers from her father. Their sweet smell wafted to her, and she felt thankful to have gotten them. They reminded her of home—her other home.

"So, I'm going to face the ring squad. Wanna catch up for lunch today?" He was looking at his arms, not her.

"Umm, actually. I should go see my mother. She'll be worried. She didn't want to come here. She's kind of anxious about…stuff." Lilah blushed a little and didn't meet his questioning gaze. "We can catch up tomorrow, though, if you don't mind it being at the bookstore. Around lunchtime?"

"Sure. I mean, if I don't make it, just know my mother made good on her threat. Otherwise, see you then." There was an awkward pause, neither wanting to say goodbye first.

She stammered, and he grunted then both looked at each other and burst out laughing.

"Okay, it got weird," Lilah admitted. "Sorry. I didn't mean for that to happen."

"Hey, it's fine. We all have our moments, right?" Peter shrugged again, and this time, she saw the tension leave his body.

She smiled. "Right. Hey, you're getting really good with Earth language now. Anyway, see you later, 'kay?" Before he could respond, she dashed out the doors and down the staircase.

She stopped at the Starling Trumpets and picked one at random for her mother. Smiling, she got all the way to the driveway before realising she didn't have a lift.

Escape

Crap...

Before panic could really set in, Seth pulled up and honked at her.

"Need a lift?" He had casual clothes and his sunnies on. Was he off work for the day? She hadn't really seen much of him. Jeff was protective, so he was always close by.

"Hey, are you playing hooky today? Where's your brother?" She looked around curiously but Jeff was nowhere to be seen.

Seth chuckled. "Nah, Jeff and Travis are away, getting things ready on Meakra. Apparently, some of the older Taylor brothers are there, and they want some help setting up the new wards, you know, for extra security. Sounded kinda boring, so I'm heading to the beach for a few hours. While it's sunny...of course." He rolled his eyes but smiled affectionately at what was obviously an instruction from Jeff.

"Ah, I see. So you are playing hooky then." She grinned at him widely.

He grinned back and tapped the passenger seat. "Get in, dork. Let's get the hell outta here for a bit. Where you headed anyway?" She clipped her safety belt as he pulled out of the carpark and into traffic. "Home."

He nodded then changed the channel on the radio. They spent the trip listening to the most recent popular songs. Some were okay, but some made them both cringe. As she got out and shut the door, she thanked him for the lift. He shrugged and told her it was no big deal, and she watched him drive up the road before turning and letting herself into the home she'd grown up in.

"Mama," she called out, but there was no reply.

Huh. Weird. She was sure someone would be here.

She raced around the house, looking in each room for her mom or Dae, her belly knotting as she went. Her anxiety was starting to peak when she heard a car door downstairs. She raced down just as her mother and brother walked into the kitchen.

Ashlyn set her groceries on the counter. "I didn't know you would be home today, my love. Oh, Dae can you put the beef into the fridge, hon? I'm not quite ready to start cooking." She enveloped her daughter in a big hug and dropped a kiss on the top of her head. "Want to stay for dinner? I'm making curry."

Lilah's belly grumbled, and she laughed.

Her mother gave her a surprised look then laughed with her. "Oh my. You're hungry. Let's get some food into your belly, hmm?" She was talking to Lilah the way she had when she was little.

Dae broke the silence by cracking a can of soda and slurping it.

When they both looked at him, he blinked innocently. "What? I'm thirsty" He held his hands out defensively, the drink threatening to spill onto the tiled floor.

"Honestly, oh child of mine." Ashlyn shook her head wearily and set about unpacking the groceries.

Both Dae and Lilah helped some, but when it became clear they were hindering more than helping, they shrugged at each other and sat at the counter. They chatted for a bit about the ball, and what had happened. It wasn't easy to discuss, so as soon as they could, they moved onto more pleasant topics.

Escape

"Sooo..." Dae began. "I hear that a certain best-friend type-person is coming to visit us soon. She says you've been ghosting her, you know."

Lilah's face lit up. "Oh my gawd, really? Amara knows I would never ghost her! That's ridiculous. Oh, that cheeky brat, I'm gonna give her a piece of my mind. When is she gonna be here? And how is it that she called you, not me?" she added sourly.

Her brother stuck his tongue out at her and took a big gulp of the soda then coughed because of the bubbles. "Well, two things. One, she did call you. I have your phone from the 'ying rat' incident the other night. *Ow*, hey, that hurt!" Ashlyn had smacked him on the arm. "Anyway, where was I? Oh, yeah. Two, I kind of texted her to say you had an accident, and that you would need help in the shop for a while. Cause, you know...recovery and all that." He gestured around then gave their mother a look that said he didn't want to be hit again.

"That didn't answer the question, though, Dae," she fumed. "When is she going to be here?"

"Now, gorgeous girl!" A high-pitched squeal came from the doorway behind her.

She spun and screamed, racing over to embrace the other woman in welcome. "I've missed you," Lilah sobbed.

"Me too. It's been way too long, Kitty. When Dae told me, I was so bloody scared. What the hell? Can't you stay out of mischief for one minute? Sheesh." She was smiling, which softened the words, and Lilah grinned like it was a big conspiracy.

The rest of the afternoon passed with giggles and chatter, even Dae joining in on the fun.

* * *

Ashlyn flitted about, preparing a huge pot of curry. She sighed as she washed off the potatoes. How wonderful this would've been with Troy here. He would've loved having all this laughter and chatter in the home. She missed her husband more now that the children were grown, and training and organising her people in secret had only helped a little. It was weird that she'd ended up being the leader of their people, but it was a sign of how respected her husband had been, and the fact that he'd trained her in the ways of war made her an asset. She was as skilled as he'd been in fighting the Huntowra.

The secret organisation that had helped hide the Aggaron were made up mostly of bureaucrats, but there were also military and national security of officers, as well as the leaders of the governments that knew of their existence. The decision to not incorporate her people with the A.S.U was her own, though. She had earned a lot of respect from the people of Earth, so they had listened to her concerns that the attack on her own world could, and probably at some point would, happen here. Especially if the Huntowra knew they were hiding the Aggaron. It wasn't fair to any of the Aggaron's allies to stay hidden, but her gut told her there was more to the attack on Helios. She'd told her trusted friends and her people that not revealing themselves was as much for everyone else's safety as it was theirs. She didn't like having to hide anything from her children, though, and Troy would've been mad that she ever had. Telling them had been a huge relief. It was the way for Aggaron to trust each other, and above all, to never lie to their loved ones.

Escape

Chapter 3

As the weeks went by, Lilah's brother vanished more often than normal, and her mother was just as secretive as she'd always been, but since learning she was in hiding, Lilah decided not to bring any attention to these facts. In fact, she often covered for them both, telling friends and co-workers that they'd been taking care of family stuff to give them space for whatever they were up to.

Things with Peter were more relaxed now. It was sometimes a little weird, much as it had been in the infirmary, but that wasn't often. They spent time just getting to know each other more, and they laughed, a lot.

The translations had been left for a while, but in the end, she voiced her thoughts on them. "They're a combination of genuine predictions with some stuff that's been added in there in a dialect that's similar but slightly different from another one. I think someone messed with it, to make it say stuff it doesn't. Or at least to make parts of it read quite differently. Taking any kind of truth from this would be hard to do. I can't decide what's genuine and what's forged. Whoever did it knew exactly what they were doing."

"So, basically what you're saying is that this is a huge waste of time and effort?" Peter sounded incredulous.

Lilah had shrugged and tried to move on, but she was curious to know more as well. The only way to do that was to finish the translations in both dialects then overlay the other four languages as well, to see all possible meanings. Perhaps that would soothe Peter's worry.

Her friendship with Ethan was a happy and strange one. They often had lunch together and would pull funny faces at each other from across the room, which resulted in them getting yelled at by her father. He'd really taken to being the boss. She'd never thought he would, but she learned that when his father had died to save everyone, Matt had seen for the first time why being an emperor was so valued. It had set him on the path to being the leader he was now, which was impressive.

Lilah felt a rush of pride and respect for him, and her heart broke a bit when she learned how after her mother and brother had died, he'd gone searching and found only his wife's body. The details sent a shiver down her spine, and she knew she would do anything to help her brother rebuild a relationship with their father.

Dae had been stubbornly refusing to be a part of the war efforts—apart from his usual scouting rosters, of course. She knew this was because of the secret, but she couldn't just announce that to everyone here. What he was doing was just as important as what the A.S.U was doing, and he'd said that having another team of soldiers ready to go was an advantage. She knew he was right, but it didn't sit well with her.

Their mother had nearly had a heart attack when she learned that Angel, a trusted ally, had been a betrayer—and a Huntowra queen, no less—and she'd own into a rage, wanting to execute the monster then and there. But common sense and a greater need to protect her entire people had prevailed. She would not kill the beast, no matter that it deserved death, and she focused even harder on training and preparing. When the

Escape

Aggaron and their allies heard that a Huntowra had made it all the way here, that it had been embedded with them, it had motivated them all to work harder to be a second line of defence. A new schedule of combat training was now almost complete, with Dae's help.

Lilah would start training with them through the Christmas holiday, but until then, it was her job to distract everyone from her brother's absence. She was the precious one, after all. As far as most were concerned, this war was already won. It didn't matter that her magix was almost completely gone, that she had no control of it. What mattered was that some prophecy had said she was dangerous and could kill all the Huntowra. The same prophecy she now knew was a pile of crap. Lies. All of it was lies. Relying on that would get them all killed if they weren't careful.

In between working with the A.S.U and her bookstore, she was seeking approval to start going on scoutings with the others. She wanted to be helpful, and she was curious about the different places she'd heard stories about. She knew now that the desert place she'd been to as a child was the Qualterra, because she'd been told about the Huntowra who'd bragged about it to his captors. He'd escaped their custody before the attack that sent everyone into hiding, but the information he'd given was accurate. So far, anyway. She was hesitant to tell anyone about the cave network, and Mierden and the others she'd trained with while there. There were so many secrets, but the thought that this war was going to be fought on many sides gave her a sense of hope that she just couldn't suppress. So, she showed up every day and went through the motions. She worked at home on the translations, to see if she could figure out what was true prophecy and what wasn't. She refused to tell Peter, though.

He'd had the biggest hissy t about it, so she had quietly set it aside then smuggled it home to work on.

On her days off, she was with her mother and Lottie, learning the healing techniques of the Aggaron and Visper, as Ashlyn had been trained by the best there was, and she started hand combat practice with Dae at home as well. She was grateful Amara had stayed, because she needed the help with her shop. She had hired her as a manager to free up time. She smiled thinking of her dear one, and how she seemed to take everything so calmly. Lilah had been sure she would freak out about the fact that her best friend was an alien, but she'd just laughed and made a joke about how it was the most logical explanation for Lilah's 'quirks.'

Today, she was hanging with Amara at the store. Peter was checking out hieroglyphs at the library. He was hoping the Egyptian ones were close enough to give him a starting point, but Lilah worried this was just him trying to bury his worries and fears now that everyone had seen a glimpse of his true power.

Setting aside her worries for him, she grabbed a couple of sandwiches and bottles of water. She was hungry lately, so she got extras in case the sandwich didn't fill her properly. She had cakes and candy—Amara had a sweet tooth— and fresh fruit salad with jelly and custard for herself. She shoved her way into the shop, using her shoulder to push the door and almost tripped over Ethan.

He was leaning against the front counter chatting animatedly to Amara, but stopped when he realised she was there. "Oh, hey. Here, let me help." He grabbed half an armful of stuff. "Gee, you aren't messing around. Whose army are you stashing this for?"

Escape

She couldn't help reacting, couldn't help her eyes widening as alarm raised the hairs on her neck. *It was a joke, Lilah. He doesn't know anything.*

Lilah took a deep breath and collected herself as best she could. "Why are you here anyway?"

Ethan shrugged. "I was lonely, figured I'd come see my best friend, and what do you think I discover? She's gone and made a new best friend. So, now I need to be best friends with both of you, and Mara and I are just getting to know each other." He rolled his eyes.

Lilah had wanted to spend some time with Amara. Her friend had called her, upset over some dreams she'd been having. Lilah wanted to ask her about them and what she thought they meant. If she was right, and there was more to this than nightmares, her friend was remembering a past life. It wasn't uncommon to find reincarnated souls where she was from, and she didn't see any reason why Earth would be different. After all, they had a strong history of magic, which seemed to Lilah to be a poor translation of magix. The ancient Gods that had roamed here were familiar to her Whistler mind, from legends of an ancient race that had tried to seize control of lesser worlds, ones easily corrupted by magix. Wouldn't it be logical to assume that this world had been targeted?

She didn't know it was fact, not yet, but she knew enough of this world's history and now she remembered lots of her own history as well. They were quite similar. If that was true, perhaps these ancients could be convinced to join forces with them against the Huntowra—assuming they were still around, of course. She was hesitant to share her thoughts, though, at least until she had solid evidence.

Lilah smiled and started to eat her egg sandwich, washing each bite down with water as she watched the banter between her best friends. They were getting along well, and she wondered brie y if Ethan would at some point feel the need to offer his hand. Amara usually didn't speak much, especially to men, but she was animated now, her eyes lit with mischief, and seemed totally relaxed. It was a wonderful lunch, and when Ethan had left, she couldn't help but think that her friend was sad.

"Hey, you doing okay there?"

"Hmm, oh. Yeah, I guess I am. It's been a big day. So, you wanted to talk some more about my dreams. I'm not sure why, though. They're not real... Right?" She was wiping the counters and reorganising the pens in the display, which had already been done that morning.

"Look, it might be nothing at all, but I got thinking. Since my memories have been coming back, I've remembered hearing about an ancient race that tried to make a run for worlds like this one. The people are more easily corrupted by magix here, and these beings had such powerful magix that even if they could use only a fraction of it, it would still cause the people here to act out. We're talking things like wars, riots... And who knows, I could just be crazy, but my gut tells me it's worth at least looking into. But if I tell my father, or anyone else, they might just think I'm nuts, or brain damaged. I trust you, Amara. Please don't say anything to anyone."

"Chill, I won't." She stared at Lilah. "I don't really know what to say. It feels kind of like I get a pulling sensation in my belly, and it halfway wakes me. Then I'm wandering the streets, only they're different. And I'm swapping stuff for food, things like cloth or jewellery. The next thing I know I'm standing in a

Escape

building that I think is home, and then a strange guy shows up. He looks at me like I'm…I don't know, less than he is and when he speaks, I get a cold shiver." She hugged herself. "So he says something about I shouldn't have hidden her from him, and then he makes a funny waving motion, and then I can't really remember much for the longest time." She sighed and got a pained look on her face. "One day, I hear a whisper. The trees all around me are swaying gently and dripping into this river I'm in. This voice, which is familiar but also somehow not, keeps saying sorry for the agony and suffering. It wants to make one tiny thing right, so it chooses to set me free…whatever that means. Then the next thing I remember, I wake up in the streets and have no clue how I got there. Nobody even knows where I'm from or if I have a family or anything." She shrugged.

Lilah was trans fixed, trying to process all the information. Were there any little details her friend could remember that would hint at where, or when, she was from? "Can you remember where you were in this dream? Or is there anything that would tell you the date, like a calendar or something?"

"No, nothing like that stands out to me, except…there were a lot of olives around. And fresh food platters. And a massive mountain, I think. It had caused earthquakes and stuff…" She pursed her lips. "Sorry. It isn't much, I know." With that, she stood and started clearing the new stock from the counters.

Lilah was lost in thought all afternoon. She was surer now that this was a reincarnation. The details were way too specific and consistent to be anything else. Where should she start, if she could start anywhere? Perhaps she needed to wait and see if any more memories surfaced, if that was what they were…

* * *

At dinner that night, Ashlyn was sporting a new bruise—well, several—but she was pleased with herself. Dae was wolfing down his dinner, and he kept his eyes on his meal. Lilah tried to talk to him, but he just grunted then went back to eating. Ashlyn watched the exchange, pulling a breadstick apart and dipping in into the soupy mixture she had made for dinner. The training was gruelling, and he'd been taking it seriously, giving his all from morning to night, every chance he got. She knew why. Her son had a father now, but he still emulated his other father, the one he'd never known other than the brief snippets she'd shared with them both. They both loved Troy as if he were their own father, but now she worried that Dae would push his biological parent away in order to fulfil some desire to be as powerful and skilled as Troy.

She would have to talk to him about it, gently remind him that although he loved his family, he needed to remember that his biological father was still here. If he ignored him for too long, he would lose another father. She ate quietly, speaking only when Lilah drew her into conversation or to pointedly get her son's opinion. He was almost diving head first into his bowl when Ashlyn decided enough was enough.

"Dae, you can help wash the dishes. Kitty, you set up the puzzle mat. We need some good old-fashioned family time." She arched her eyebrow when Dae opened his mouth to argue, and he snapped it shut again, nodding.

* * *

Escape

They stood as one and set about their chores. Lilah headed into the library to clear off the ancient desk they used for games and puzzling. Soft talking came from the kitchen, which backed onto the library, and she stopped to try to hear them better. Eavesdropping wasn't really her favourite thing to do, but she didn't think they would speak so freely in front of her. They'd both become extra paranoid about security, and if she were being honest with herself, she was worried about more traitors among the staff at A.S.U as well. She just refused to let the fear consume her every waking moment.

After a minute of muted chatter, though, she gave up. She couldn't make out anything. When they were ready, she was sure they would tell her what was going on. She just didn't like feeling left out. She was picking up some random books when she saw the copy of dragon stories Peter had given her weeks ago. She smiled warmly. She'd felt so odd seeing the cover, as though she knew the dragon on it. Peter told her the legends said it was Mirren's dad, Mierden. She paused for a moment then a flash of memory hit her like a wave crashing onto the sand.

The giant stairs went on and on, twisting upwards. She was tired, but the screeches here didn't seem to like them; they never went here. She was curious and had nothing else to do here, wherever here was. After a long time, the stairs opened onto a huge square floor with towers all round it. The towers were covered with pretty images and symbols, and she was drawn to them. She walked slowly, since it was empty, touching the images here and there as she did. When she reached the back, she saw a giant set of double doors, bigger than even the roof. They looked ancient, and they had some shimmery webs on them.

P Ryall

Who used these doors? They had to be really big if they needed them that tall. As she leaned closer to them, the doors creaked open. She jumped back, wanting to run away, but she was curious about who, or what, was in there. As the doors swung more fully open, they revealed a room. It was dark, and it smelled bad, but she went in anyway.

The giant doors shut gently behind her, and she blinked a few times, trying to get her eyes used to the darkness. As the doors sealed with a *thunk*, tiny popping sounds came from all sides of the room. Fires sprang up in wells that ran along the walls and went down another stairway. It was as large as the one she'd climbed to get up here, and she sat on the stone floor for a minute in frustration. Finally, she sighed. She'd come this far; she may as well just keep going. Maybe there was a way out at the bottom.

She gingerly made her way down, being as quiet as she could in case there was someone…or something here. She finally made it to a flattened floor, but…this wasn't a way out. It went further in. This was an enormous underground room, and the only path was the one directly in front of her. She stepped onto the dirt passageway then backtracked immediately. A gust of air swirled around the cavernous room, and res exploded into life all around her.

This wasn't just a room. It was a cave with entrances all over the place, but mostly up higher than any person could reach. Was there a secret ladder or something? A low grumbling began from below, and she looked down in horror as she realised this cave didn't have a bottom. From the depths of this pit, several shapes were coming upwards, towards her. She cowered against the wall as twelve giant dragons unfurled into the spaces, the

Escape

ones she'd assumed were entries. They snarled as they smelled the intruder in their midst.

She was instantly fascinated, and she watched as they appeared to hold a conversation in their language. She was almost able to make out the gist of it, the owing sounds pitching and rolling like a melody. A very growly melody, but still. Curiosity drew her cautiously forward, being careful to not make sudden moves or noises. Before she knew it, she was nearly halfway across the narrow dirt path. She jumped in terror when a deep voice spoke.

"Who are you, youngling?" The voice was soft, yet a chill went up her spine.

She looked around her in a panic, sweat beading on her forehead. "Umm, I'm…"

Her jaw dropped. Directly in front of her was the whitest, oldest, and scariest dragon she'd ever seen. His tail was swishing around, its three razor prongs slicing the air. His horns, constantly twisting, looked like they were made of gold, matching his liquid golden eyes, which flickered like the flames. Looking at his horns was like watching a tree move and grow in fast motion. Terri ed, excited, she stood there, wordless.

"Why aren't you answering my question? That's very rude. And how is it you came to be in here? All the others are in Halla, getting ready. This nether-space is not a safe place to dwell, even for a short time. We are not the only beings that inhabit this pocket world. Come, and I will return you to the others."

She panicked, letting out a scream that was almost inaudible. Surely, he didn't mean the screeches? She didn't want to be out there again, alone. She was hungry, and scared, and cold. She stood there shivering, and her belly let out a loud growl of its own.

The ancient white dragon looked at her for a moment then cocked his head. "Your belly growls as loud as a dragon. Those in Halla do not allow the younglings to go unnourished. Have you been lost here?" His words softened slightly.

She took a deep breath. "I don't know. I was in the scary place, and there were lots of screeches, and I can't find food. I was all alone when I woke up in a pod thing. I found the stairs when I stopped hiding inside the caves and decided to hide here instead." She brushed her hair back from her face and scrubbed tears from her cheek. She was so cold now her hands felt like ice. "My tummy hurts, and I'm really thirsty." She felt dizzy suddenly and swayed before everything went dark.

She woke in a brightly coloured eld with a tall, muscular man standing near her, talking to the white dragon. "I've never seen this youngling before today, and I always make it a priority to know everyone here. This child isn't from here, I'm afraid." He had a kind voice, and his shoulder-length hair shone in the sunshine.

"I'm sorry, Dale, we cannot allow her back into the Qualterra. It's miraculous she even made it into the nether-space. The Huntowra are patrolling, so trying to find her people right now would be a bad idea. We are all at risk if they find us. We mustn't be caught, or we will all perish." He sighed heavily as he sat down. The ground trembled slightly.

Dale smiled gently and stroked his short beard. He was staring at nothing, clearly thinking. His arms were strong, with many bands, and his sword had been well used. The hilt was

Escape

frayed in places, and there was a talisman attached to the end. She wondered what it was, or what it meant.

"Poor child. Well, we will care for her here for as long as needed. She can train with the other younglings when she's able. In the meantime, I'll have the healer Kayla see to her. She looks starved and dehydrated. She will be weak for some time yet, I fear, but with regular meals and water, she will recover." He was thoughtful then as he glanced at her.

Seeing her awake, he winked.

She smiled and blinked at him, not able to wink one eye.

"You have extensive medical knowledge, Dale. Were you perhaps a healer in your previous life?" the old dragon wondered.

Dale barked out a laugh. "Heck no. Well, I don't think so. Have you seen me wield my sword?" He gestured to the sword she'd just been admiring.

The old dragon gave him a disparaging look. "Yes. I've seen it." With that, he got up and stretched out his wings.

They were as stunning underneath as above, with a fine fur that shimmered and fluffed out. She wanted to touch his wings, just to see it they were as soft as they looked, but she couldn't move. He gracefully arched his back, and with an almighty ap, launched into the air. The suddenness of it made Dale stagger sideways and chuckle.

"Pesky great one thinks he knows it all," he muttered to himself.

* * *

P Ryall

A loud crash snapped Lilah back to the present, and she dashed to the kitchen to see what had happened. When she rounded the corner, she skidded to a halt. The sight of her mother and brother laughing threw her off balance.

"Oh my gosh, what happened? I heard an almighty crash. I was really worried." She bit her lower lip to stop it from trembling.

Dae looked at her seriously for a minute then howled with laughter again, the ferocity of it doubling him over. Their mother smacked him playfully, clearly in on the joke.

Lilah just huffed and stormed back into the library, folding her arms in front of her as she plopped into the plush armchair. As she sat there scowling, she thought about the memory she'd just had. Dale. He'd become a father figure to her, and she worried now for his wellbeing. She couldn't remember how she'd come to be here, alone, but she knew he would be looking for her. Poor Dale, and all the others she'd met there in Halla. She wouldn't tell her loved ones. She had to protect them at all costs.

When they came in a few minutes later, Dae was carrying their usual hot cocoa, and Ashlyn had a tray of brownies, still warm from the oven. Lilah glanced at them and quickly away. They didn't seem to notice that she was nervous. She launched into sorting the pieces of the puzzle they were working on, giving her brother one collection while their mother dished the brownies and set about sorting out another pile of pieces. This was something they did often, and it helped them to work around each other without arguments. She started humming a lullaby, one Dale used to hum a lot.

Escape

Ashlyn's hand froze mid-air, the blood draining from her face as she stared at her daughter. "Kitty." She sounded like she had sandpaper in her throat. "Where did you hear that?"

Lilah shrugged. "It was the lullaby my friend used to sing to me, in the other place. Before I was here, but ages after I was stolen from Meakra. Dale looked after me for a few years and taught me how to fight some. He was teaching lots of people to fight. He's my friend, but he's more like a dad to me too. I just remembered him."

Ashlyn gave her a stern look and her brother seemed thoughtful, but they let it drop and enjoyed the rest of the evening quietly puzzling.

Lilah and Dae stayed at their mother's house for the night. It was late—or early, depending how you looked at it — when they finally went to bed. They were yawning all the way upstairs, and when she reached her room, Lilah was too tired to even change into her nightie. She flopped onto the soft, squishy mattress facedown, fully clothed, and fell asleep instantly. She dreamed of colours and flying. Food that made her want to eat even though her tummy wanted to pop from being so full, and Dale, looking in desert wastelands for her and panicking when she was nowhere to be found.

Chapter 4

Amara and Lilah loved to stay busy, and now that she was well again, Lilah wanted adventures—and not the imaginary ones either. Between the healing sessions with Eva and gaining back some of her memories, Lilah felt bored and helpless sitting around. Peter had been off world a lot lately, helping as much as he could. But he also tried to be with her as much as possible. The eternal bands meant they missed each other so fiercely they actually hurt when they were separated. It wasn't that bad when they knew where the other one was and how long it would be until they were together again, but it was a little unsettling being so tightly bound to another being this way.

"If we go to a travel agent, we can book one of those mystery holidays, Mara. We just tell them what type of holiday we want, they build it to our budget, and off we go. It's a really exciting way to travel, don't you think?" Lilah was thumbing through lea et after lea et.

"Fine, but only cause it's with you. And this mystery holiday, my terms are that it must be somewhere neither of us has ever been, there needs to be lots of fresh foods available, and it must have some kind of historical importance. Deal?" She held out her thin hand to shake, and Lilah took it with a grin.

They spent the morning talking about the different places they'd been, writing them down so the travel agent could cross

Escape

them from their list of possible destinations. Then they made some phone calls. Amara talked to Ashlyn so they could organise for her to run the bookstore for two weeks, and Lilah phoned and asked the A.S.U to give her some time off before her duties really started, so she could be fully rested and ready to work as soon as she got back. They agreed, mostly because her roaming this world was more desirable than other ones, where a stray beast or Huntowra could attack her.

It was a perk of being a princess, she supposed, and though she hated it as a general rule, she was inclined to use her status this one time to try to ferret out information about her friend's dreams. Or memories. Lilah was determined that magix had at some point existed here. Maybe still did. She just had to prove it. She couldn't even really say why she felt so strongly about it, just that she knew it was true and might be important for them all.

* * *

Dae had been hard on everyone around him these last few weeks. Seeing his sister attacked and being helpless to stop it had really affected him. He had to get stronger. He needed to be able to protect his family at all costs. The aftermath of that night haunted him. When Peter had done…whatever he'd done, Dae had completely frozen. He'd been sure his sister was dead. She'd been so lifeless there in the magix ring. Then the whole room exploded, and both were gone from this world. His friend and his sister. He'd been having nightmares since it happened, and he channelled it into his new training regime.

Ashlyn had him doing basic stuff like building his endurance and practicing his shooting skills, but she was also teaching him the ways of the Aggaron. To tap into a primal part of his being that allowed him to shut down his fear and think in a logical and calculating way. It involved a lot of meditation techniques mingled with small amounts of magix that rewrote his basic survival instincts as it relaxed him.

Then there was the hand-to-hand combat with opponents who had all the advantages as well as sword training. Troy had been the best of the best and had trained his wife just so they could spend time together. She, in turn, had taught him everything she knew about medicine and healing. Dae wished he'd known how experienced she was as a healer. She was a prodigy according to their closest friend, Lottie, and that was why she was now the leader of the Aggaron.

When he thought about it, it scared him that she hadn't been able to help Lilah. What that meant was his sister's illness was worse than he'd ever thought possible. He was shocked to learn that Ashlyn, and others of their kind, had tried everything to defeat this mystery illness. Ashlyn had been hard with him about his training, but he didn't mind. He wanted this more than anything.

Then there was his other problem: his biological father. He wanted to connect with his children, but Dae was scared. He also worried that he would lose him...again. If he let himself get close to Matt in more than a professional way, he was open to being hurt again, and that wasn't something he wanted. Besides, how could they have a relationship when Dae didn't even remember the man? He felt weird. On one hand, he craved the link a biological family offered...not to mention a father. On the other hand, he was a complete stranger. The leader of a people Dae wasn't even allowed to speak to. But his mother had told him off for not trying to connect with his father, and he'd promised her he would try.

Escape

The meeting room was empty except for cleaners, so maybe now was a good time to go looking for Matthew. Or should he try again later? He didn't even know what to say. This would be so bloody awkward. The anxiety was so strong it hurt to breathe. Just as he'd nearly talked himself into cancelling this impromptu visit, doors from the upper floor opened and he heard talking. Should he run for it now or find some reason to go when they came into sight? Argh… this was torture.

As it turned out, he didn't need to worry. It was a group of younger scouts who'd been standing guard on Meakra, and they didn't really notice him, not even sparing him a glance as they went by. He didn't know them personally, but he knew they were the only team that should be here today. He'd checked. He shrugged and decided to go see if his friends were here. He'd start with the library. Peter would be there, surely. He hadn't seen much of him since…everything, and he wasn't sure how to discuss it either. What had happened was rare, like super rare, and he was curious about how he'd done it. Nobody else here had that kind of magix, not even the Huntowra queen.

When he got to the library, he casually strolled through the doors but then stopped dead in his tracks.

Fuck. He was here. He stayed out of sight to listen, wanting to get a clearer understanding of what his father was like.

"No, that isn't what I asked, dammit. You know what I mean, Peter. I think we need to get you to Meakra so we can do a new power read. There must be an explanation for why your magix is so different. There are stories in the palace vault of an ancient race who had magix similar to this. It's possible some of us out there are their descendants. We need to look into it. And besides, you're one of the most talented warriors we have.

Spending all your time here in this dusty place is a waste. Either way, I'd feel better knowing you were there, where you can help our warriors and Evaliah can give you a thorough check-up."

"I'm not some super security guy, and my talents are better used here. I like my *dusty place* by the way. And, oh yeah...who's going to tell Lilah? She won't stand for this, and you know it. The pain of being separated, it isn't something either of us wants to feel any more than necessary. So, if you order me to go, and I guess you can, seeing as you're the emperor, just know that she'll go as well. Is that what you really want, Matt?"

Dae knew that the answer was no, he didn't want that at all. None of them did. Keeping her safe was his—their— main goal right now.

"Christ. No. Of course I don't want her there, not until the area is safe and heavily guarded, at least. This is just so important. We need to have as many warriors there as we can. The buggers tried to ambush our guys again. Trenton was hurt. It wasn't irreparable, but still...I feel like we need to do more. I want to protect them all. I wish I could without putting anyone in danger..."

"I'll help." He hadn't meant to speak, but the words were out before he realised it.

Matthew swung around to see who'd spoken, his jaw nearly hitting the floor when he realised it was Damian. He was shaking his head in denial, but Dae cut off anything he might have said.

"I am a warrior. I trained with the best here on Earth, and it's in my blood as well." He smirked at his father. "And you said

Escape

it yourself: we need all the help we can get to prepare this base. Seems to me I'm as good a choice as the next guy, right?"

"Damon, I—"

"With all due respect, *sir*, it's Damian. Dae for short." "Okay, yeah. Sorry. Dae, you're the crown prince. Sending you there unprotected is as dangerous as sending your sister. If anything happens to me…"

"She can inherit your job…and title. I am not going to sit here while you send the people I care about off on some death mission. And Peter's practically my brother-in-law too. Kitty would skin me if I let him get sent off alone."

"Kitty?" Matthew blinked in confusion. "Sorry, who's Kitty?"

"That's what he calls Lilah, Matt." Peter spoke softly.

The older man gave a nod of understanding. "Ah, I see. Kitty. That's a pretty nickname." He sighed. "Fine. You win. I'll go chat to Tobias and organise for you to be re-rostered for missions. Is that acceptable to you?" He glanced at his son with a look that could only be described as sarcastic.

Dae paused a moment then decided to be as formal. "Yep, and no special treatment. If any dudes get in my way while I'm working, they risk getting shot." He spun on his heel and left without a backward glance.

* * *

"Humph," Matthew grumbled. "Does he realise he does that when he leaves a room?" He jabbed a thumb in the direction his son had headed off in.

Peter laughed. "Sorry," he coughed out between chortles. "I literally just thought the same thing about you a few weeks back. It's funny that you say it about your son. Guess it's genetic." He dragged his fingers across his scruffy chin.

He needed a shave. Not that he cared much about facial hair, but it was annoying when he was eating.

The conversation turned to lighter topics then, and after a short time Matthew left to attend to business.

* * *

Lilah booked the mystery holiday for her and Amara during lunch and was given instructions on what to pack for the adventure. The flier she'd been emailed was purposely vague, but basically, they were to pack for all possible weather events and take an extra case to bring home any goods they purchased.

Amara was uttering about, serving customers and tidying as she went. She was straightening some history books when one caught her eye. She paused then opened the book with a curious expression on her face.

Lilah saw it but was instantly distracted.

"Hey." Seth looked like he'd been blown about by a giant fan or something, his hair sticking up weirdly and his shirt partially unbuttoned. "Whatcha doin?"

She laughed. It amazed her how quickly they'd become friends, and she was glad she'd met him. "Oh Seth. You're a goose, did you know that?"

"Cool, I like birds. Always figured I'd be an eagle or something, but hey, a goose will do." He gave her a huge cheeky grin, and they laughed together for a moment. "Are you guys

Escape

busy now? I was about to do a Chinese food run, figured I'd see if you wanted anything while I'm there." He shrugged absently.

She thought for a moment. "Sure, get us…Actually, you know what? Surprise us. You choose. We're in the mood to experience things we haven't before, and this is just one thing we can say we did. Surprise take-out meals." She grinned at him again, and Amara made her way over.

"Nice smiles. What did you do?" she said seriously to Lilah then burst out laughing at her friend's expression. "Kidding, duh." She rolled her eyes.

"Seth's gonna get us a mystery dinner! I was saying we're in the mood to experience something different and he's on his way to get takeaway. So, win-win."

* * *

"Yeah, figured it would save you both from forgetting to eat, again. If I have to have someone fuss over me, I sure as hell am gonna fuss over my friends when I can." He stared at Amara.

Was she okay? She looked kind of scared or something.

She shrugged and nodded but didn't speak, and he decided not to press the issue. Surely Lilah knew whatever it was that was upsetting her. It was none of his business.

He left then, thinking they would like some kung pao chicken and sautéed vegetables with flavoured rice and a sour soup. The restaurant he was going to made the best food, but they didn't have much money to advertise, so they were virtually unknown. He only knew about it because as a street kid he'd wandered to their bins looking for scraps and the owner Tan had caught him.

P Ryall

At first, the elderly man looked like he was going to beat him soundly, but the moment he saw the chicken carcass Seth had shed out, his eyes welled. He told Seth that in return for some basic cleaning, he would give him a hot meal. Tan insisted that he couldn't ex and bend like he needed to, so this was the perfect solution for them both. It was a crock of shit, of course, but he was grateful for the old man's kindness. Travis and his father had also been a major blessing, but this moment was etched in his mind forever.

He would swing by every couple of days and do some cleaning, always trying to do more to show appreciation; and the old man would load him up with three large containers full to bursting with food and soups. He had complained it was too much, but the old geezer had brushed it off, saying he had cooked too much and wasn't allowed to sell it after a certain time. Nowadays, Seth went in at every opportunity, and Tan welcomed him like a son.

The chime on the door gently tinkled as he went in. It was a little busier than usual tonight, and he soon realised why. About half the staff members from work were here, including Trav and Jeff. They were tucked away in a corner, trying to remain separate from the others, but it was clear they were part of the group. Travis saw Seth and waved him over, just as Tan made his way out of the kitchens. He rushed to Seth and hugged him while bowing his head repeatedly in thanks.

"What's happened here, T-man?" he asked.

"You tell everyone that Tan makes best food, now everyone wants best food." He was beaming with pride, the smile on his face so huge it was nearly scary.

Escape

Seth didn't think he had anything to do with the increase of customers, but he was glad the old man was finally getting some well-deserved publicity. Seth was grateful for Travis, who'd clearly told everyone about Tan's. He made his way to the buffet area and was scooping up his choices when Tan sidled up to him.

"Why you get takeaway? Is Tan's too busy today?" He was so sincere, Seth just shook his head with a smile.

"No, that's not it at all, T. I promised two ladies who are working hard that I would bring them the best dinner ever. Of course, that means that I need to do takeaway." He shrugged and continued to scoop.

"Why do that? Tan will bring the shop to them. Come, we need burners and pots. I will gather ingredients and we will go to them. They have a fresh and hot best meal ever." He rushed out back to give instructions loudly to the other staff.

Before Seth had time to even replace the ladle, Tan was back with the biggest backpack he'd ever seen. They drove the ten minutes back to the bookstore, Tan holding onto all the ingredients and talking about how he was trying a new Peking duck recipe soon. He hoped it would bring in more customers; they seemed to like duck.

The front door was locked when they got there, but Lilah opened it excitedly when she saw him.

* * *

"Oh wow, this is amazing! I didn't know Chinese restaurants did an at-home dining experience. That's so cool. Do you take bookings for events? I can hand out fliers if you have any. My mother *loves* Chinese food. This would perfect for her at the company."

"We don't normally do bookings, but for Seth's friends, I will do booking." He bowed graciously and got to work.

He handed Amara a ask when she sat at the table, and she took it curiously. "What is it?"

"That is Tan's sour soup. My own family recipe, from my father's father."

"Ooh, that sounds good. Thank you." She unscrewed the lid.

A pungent citrus smell wafted on the air, and all their bellies growled. Amara poured some into a small bowl set in front of her by Tan, and she passed it to Seth. They ate their dinner right there in front of the counter, books all around them. It really was the best Chinese food. Lilah was excited to set up a meal like this for Peter. His curiosity about this world and all the cultures here meant he wanted all the experiences he could get.

It was nearly eleven PM when the dinner and conversation finally finished, and the girls locked up with huge grins and giggles.

"Okay, it was an epic experience." Amara rolled her eyes as she admitted it.

"I loved it. What an amazing way to have takeaway. To have them come to you is awesome. I wonder where he got the idea from." Lilah was adding padlocks to the security screens. There'd been some vandals around recently, and she wasn't taking any chances.

Escape

Amara fidgeted with her bag uncomfortably. "I think people did that wherever I lived. I sort of remember my father had people call on us, and they always had platters and stuff."

"Well, hopefully one day we can find your family. Seems to me you've started getting some memories. That's a good sign."

"I don't think so, Kitty. In fact, I'm starting to think this magic thing is real, and that I was somehow ripped away from my family by it. My head's all messed up, and I don't want to get into the details, but I really think that if it's true what you say, these beings won't want to help fight the bad guys. Well, one would. Maybe two. But not the others." She was nearly in tears, and Lilah wrapped her in a hug, assuring her it was going to be okay.

Secretly, she was worried that Amara was right. If they were who she thought, they likely wouldn't help even if they were still around.

Chapter 5

MEAKRA

Peter was exhausted, and he smelled. Bad. The bathrooms on Meakra weren't usable yet, and he was covered in giant bug goop. He'd gone on a scheduled trip, at Matthew's request, of course. Dae was annoyed about it, sensing his father had something to do with it. Peter had felt guilt and shame for agreeing to spy on him, so he'd made the excuse that Lilah was going to be mad if he'd allowed Dae to go without at least offering to come with him.

He'd thought about that for a few minutes then grumbled. "Yeah, that sounds about right. I suppose it's good that you're here anyway. I wanted to ask you about...well, you know. That night. I guess I was kinda curious to know what happened, and why everyone freaked out. I mean, I don't have memories to answer it all for me," he finished in a low whisper.

Peter nodded, scrubbing his hands over the back of his neck. He'd known this was going to happen. He just hadn't counted on his friend not knowing why people were so upset with him. It made things easier, actually. He had an opportunity to fully explain himself to someone who had no way to judge him. He decided then to tell him everything. All of it, even the bits Lilah had been hiding. She would want that.

"Okay, I'll do my best to explain it to you. But I have a condition...well, two, actually. One, what I say to you is in

Escape

confidence and goes nowhere else. It stays between us. Two. Hear it all, and don't judge. You can't possibly know just how complex…how scary and really confusing it all is." When his friend nodded, he went on. "This is a long tale, Dae, and I won't talk about it right here with all these ears. Meet me after everyone's eaten and retired for the night. I brought some mead from the stores back at headquarters, so we can discuss this with a drink…or three." He grimaced at the other man then turned away.

He needed to get to the vault today. Matthew had promised him access to see if there was anything about his strange powers in the histories that had been removed from the public's eye during the great cleansing some thousand years before. It had always been their intention to release the history, but then the Huntowra war had begun, and it had been forgotten.

He walked the halls of the palace absently; he knew them as well as his own home on Haven. *Haven.* Oh, how he missed it there. He glanced up at the sky, at the bright orb that had been his home. It glowed gently in the afternoon light. It was so close, he'd wondered if the trees there would colour the surface. They didn't, but still it was nice to imagine.

As he turned the corner of the eastern hall, he spied the old cottage on the edges of the forest. Starling Trumpets overgrew the whole gardens in every colour of the rainbow, and just behind the cottage was the tree. It had tendrils that had grown into Earth's magix ring now, but the original tree was firmly rooted here. The branches stretched out quietly, and the leaves were a deep green with light green veins that almost glowed. He couldn't see the veins from here, but he could tell that the leaves were drooping, because Lilah wasn't here to restore them to health. The silver berries bloomed but were dulled to an almost grey. She must've been days from death, for the berries to be so dull. Of course, the fact the tree had fruited at all was a miracle. It hadn't done that after her abduction, which was why they'd believed she had died. When Peter had connected the tree to her via the new one, it had apparently restored this one somewhat.

He was looking at the tree when footsteps rushed toward him, and he spun around to see why anyone would be running here. A child, no more than ten, came to a sudden halt at the sight of Peter standing in the path. A few more seconds, and three of the scouts caught up, clearly puffed from chasing the boy. He looked terrified, quickly casting his gaze between the three chasers and himself.

It was hard to say if the child was more afraid of them or him, and with Peter in his armour, he must've looked even scarier than usual. The child was thin. It seemed like he hadn't eaten for a while, and in his hands were some ready to-eat meals, clearly stolen. His eyes still darted around, and he was panting, dragging in deep, ragged breaths then huffing them out quickly.

"Hey, it's okay, kid. Have you got any parents?" Peter spoke loud enough to drown out the scouts.

The boy stared at him wide-eyed, so Peter gave him a look he hoped was friendly and concerned. "Nah, no. It's just me, and my sister. We haven't eaten for a while, so I made a portal and came looking for something to eat.

She's...she's hiding."

"Why is she hiding? What happened?"

"The winged monsters came to our home. We thought they were gonna trade for food and stuff. That's what they said

Escape

anyway. And then one night, everyone was asleep and there were these huge noises. We woke up, and they were everywhere, dragging us all out of our homes. They killed heaps of us and laughed about it. Some they set free, but then they hunted them after a while. I took my sister, and we just hid in the caves, and when it went quiet, we tried to find dad, but when we did…" His voice, barley a whisper now, broke, and tears streamed down his cheeks as his whole body shook. One of the ration packs clanged to the floor and he jumped, clearly terrified.

"Listen to me, okay? My name is Peter, and we aren't going to hurt you. We're fighting the Huntowra, the ones you call winged ones. They're destroying all the worlds they can. Nowhere is safe from them right now. Except where we are staying, with those people on their planet." He pointed to the scouts then continued. "Let's go get your sister so you can both come to where we're staying. We'll get both of you food, and clothes." When the boy still hesitated, he went on softly, "I need you to trust me on this, okay?"

"Kay," he mumbled, rubbing his eyes with one arm. "Only cause you look real scary. The bad creatures will probably run away from you."

Peter smiled wryly and nodded.

After translating for the scouts, he led the boy to the informal parlour area and they opened the portal together, using the boy's magix.

* * *

As soon as the portal started to close, he knew this place was unsafe. For starters, the air hung heavy with the smell of re, and blood. The metallic smell was unmistakable. As they looked ahead in the early evening, they saw mounds strewn all round, as far as the eye could see. They weren't clear from a distance, but he assumed these were wheat or grain, ready for trading. Peter sucked in a deep breath and looked at his new friend. The boy was silently crying. The tears left streaks on his face, and his eyes seemed to lose their colour. Hmm, was this boy from some kind chameleon species?

He looked at Peter and gulped. "Who's gonna bury them?" His voice cracked and he started crying in earnest.

Peter blinked stupidly. *Them*. And then it dawned on him: these were not balled-up mounds of produce. These were people. Bodies. *Fuck*.

"Oh. Argh, oh god. I'm sorry. How do I... I mean, what do I..." The words didn't come. He was in shock, and his brain felt disconnected from his body.

People, more than he'd ever seen before, and all wiped out. Gone. Tears threatened to spill, and he coughed, trying to hold them in. Trying not to just drop to his knees and bawl like an infant right here on this hellish spot.

No, the boy needed him to stay strong. He squared his shoulders and took a long breath in. "Do you have a name, kid?"

"Aker. My name's Aker. My sister is this way." He pointed off to the west and started to head off, leaving Peter to stand there for a second before realising he was supposed to be following.

He caught up with Aker quickly, his long strides eating up the distance without effort. The boy gave him a cursory glance then went back to leading. It was a fair hike. They headed up into the mountains then veered into a hidden valley not visible from the air. The trees here were so dense it was almost

Escape

pitch black. There was a small winding trail gently lit by small floating lanterns. Would they give away their position?

"Were the lights your idea, Aker?"

"The lights weave all throughout our world, and they have many false trails. If you wander off here and take a wrong turn, you could be lost forever to the wilds. We all study the correct path from a very young age, and we are guided by the spirit masters. They whisper to us if there is danger ahead or following behind. The winged ones somehow fooled the spirit masters, and so we trusted them. I wish they had listened to the light goddess. She sees the truth in her eyes before the truth is known. It was she who said I would meet a strong warrior, and that he would help me to restore the Cateju. I think that's you, so I'm trusting you." He gave Peter a stern look that was heartbreaking and slightly scary all at once.

Peter nodded solemnly. How this child had suffered. He deserved to be a boy again, not be forced into manhood by this atrocity. Though if he were honest, the damage was already done. He'd seen too much and heard things no child ever should.

There were some slight flapping sounds above. What kind of ying creature lived here? It sounded about the size of a cave dragon. His ears were highly sensitive to sound so he imagined the animal was some distance away. If it got closer, he would say something.

"Nearly there now. She was hurt, so I couldn't just run away with her. I don't know how to make her better though." Aker wrung his hands anxiously.

"That's ne. We can get her to a healer. We'll also have you checked for wounds while we're at it, okay?" He narrowed his eyes, and the boy nodded, his shoulders relaxing.

P Ryall

As they rounded another corner, the path opened into a small meadow surrounded by several other paths. A slightly higher a network of caves dotted the face of a cliff he hadn't seen at first—it was onyx with a slight shimmer to the face. One of the caves had a dim light coming from within, and it was this one they headed for.

Inside the cave, there was enough room for maybe four small people, but Peter had to stoop to stop his head from hitting the roof. Aker ran to the far back corner of the cave, where his sister was curled in some skins. When she realised he was there, she threw her arms round his neck and pushed her tiny face into his shoulder.

"Aker, I was so worried about you. You were gone for a long time, and the spirit masters said I had to stay quiet and hide. It isn't safe here. I'm scared, Aker!" She wailed and shook, still holding tight to her brother.

"Shhhh, it's okay now, Kyala. We're not staying here. We must go. Soon. Here, we brought food, and then our new friend Peter will help us go somewhere safe for us. Okay?" He rocked her gently, and she eyed the big man warily. She nodded, though, and for some reason, that made Peter relax, as if he'd been holding his breath. Her brother helped her to a sitting position and, as he turned and left to get her some fresh water and a ration pack, Peter saw her stomach. All of it. She'd been eviscerated. A gash ran from one side of her to the other, and though there were rags pressed to her wounds, it was clear her internal organs were not inside her body. She was a baby. How was she not screaming? Or dead? He sucked in a sharp breath and rushed to her. He needed to help this child, *now*.

"Let me see the wounds, little one. We're going to get you to a proper healer as soon as your brother returns, okay?"

Escape

She nodded, wide eyed and pale.

Peter examined the wounds. Some kind of herbal mixture coated the rags pressed to her stomach. As he pulled his hand away, his fingertips tingled then went completely numb. *Hmm, interesting.* This was more effective than anaesthetic. He didn't have a chance to ask about it, though. There was a loud scream from just outside followed by the unmistakable howl of a Huntowra.

He shouted, "Stay" to Kyala and was outside before he even registered moving.

The Huntowra had pinned Aker down at a well in the middle of the meadow, his claw piercing the boy's chest. Peter ran as fast as he could but just as he reached them, an unearthly rip rent the air and the boy stopped screaming. Shit. Peter raised his hand, and bright light emerged, blasting the Huntowra with an enormous shockwave that also destroyed half the mountain, causing the rocky ground to quiver and trees to topple for a good kilometre.

He stared open-mouthed for a second then his brain snapped out of it, and he spun to the boy. He was still. Too still, and too quiet. Peter knelt and began to work quickly, trying to stop the bleeding, but in the end all he could do was cover the wounds with the same rags the other child had on.

Peter gathered the girl in his arms, telling her that her brother had been hurt so they had to get somewhere safe right away. She nodded wordlessly and held onto his neck. When he gathered Aker up, he was grateful for the first time that his secret was out, and he opened a portal to A.S.U without needing any focus at all.

Chapter 6

EARTH
Peter stood in the meeting room and stared at all the people staring in horror at him. Then he realised he must have looked really bad, and with two severely injured children bundled into his arms...

"We need medical here *now*!" he boomed.

Everyone started running. Some to him and the little ones, and some to the infirmary. Within minutes, they had the children on their way to theatre, and he was telling them everything he could about what had happened, the stuff on his hand that was really potent, and the attack.

"I'm supposed to be a guard for the palace restoration team, but this kid looked so scared. Can someone find my brother and tell him to replace me there for now? I'll be back when I know the kids are okay."

"Which brother?" someone asked. He didn't know or care who.

"Any of them. They all owe me," he snapped, and the person took off to find a Taylor brother.

Peter paced as the trauma team worked on the children. After what seemed like forever, he felt a twinge in his left wrist. *Lilah*. She would've felt his agitation, so of course she would find him. He felt a wave of sadness as she drew closer and

Escape

worked hard to control his emotions. On top of the expected trauma of what he'd witnessed, he had anxiety about his accidental power explosion. He wasn't sure what to make of it yet. What he needed was to know these kids were okay so he could go and talk to Matthew.

The vault was still sealed, so any useful info in there wasn't in danger. They could save that for another day. He wanted to talk about what was happening with his magix now. Matt had only seemed surprised for a short time and then he'd easily accepted that Peter was different but not a threat to them. His own mother had been much less gracious about it all. She'd thrown things and yelled for hours on end, even accused him at one point of being some kind of imposter. It stung him to even think about that right now, but he brushed it off as Lilah quietly let herself into the waiting room.

She had an armful of stuff with her—some food and two coffees—balancing them all precariously as she wound through the scattered chairs and ottomans. He watched her, completely mesmerised by the way she seemed to oat around obstacles. When she reached him, she smiled, handed him a coffee cup and sandwich then made herself comfortable on a small plush couch. There were no words. She just stayed and let him be in his own head. It was the most comforting thing he'd ever experienced.

He went back to thinking of his new ability and pacing. He concentrated on the steps, watching his feet and trying to force his mind to make sense of all that was happening.

"Ah, here you are. I've been looking for you. Hello, Lilah." Eva smiled at her then looked back at Peter. "They're both in recovery now. The little girl is doing better than her brother. Surprisingly, the herbs Aker treated her with were much more effective than most remedies I know. However, she has a major infection and the surgeons here removed part of her bowels because they'd been left exposed for too long. They say she'll need some strict dietary care, but she's expected to make a full recovery. For the time being, they've placed her into an induced coma, to help her tiny body start the healing process. Unfortunately, there isn't much I can do for her. Healing with magix is always limited anyway and here... well, it's all the harder."

"And Aker? How is he?"

"Very lucky to be here at all. Whatever you did somehow saved his life."

"That Huntowra tried to rip his lungs out of his chest. I only stuffed the wounds with those rags he had for his sister. I didn't do anything useful there today, Eva."

"That's not true. You got rid of the Huntowra, and his chest wound had started to seal somehow. This isn't any kind of magix he has. This was you. You healed the wound enough to keep him alive to get him here. I think there's much to your abilities yet to discover. And I, for one, am excited at the thought that you have new and more potent ways of healing. I would very much like to learn from you. Assuming we can duplicate the process, of course." She ducked her head, and he suddenly felt embarrassed.

She wanted him to teach her. He hadn't done anything to the boy, had he? He thought. When the Huntowra had been blasted back, he'd rushed forwards and placed his hand on Aker's chest—trying to stop the bleeding—and he'd thought he just needed him to hang in there a little longer. As he'd turned to go get the rags so he could stem the blood ow, his hand had warmed slightly. Could that have been it? He wasn't sure, but he

Escape

told Eva all he could. If he'd done anything, it hadn't been deliberate, and he was fairly sure he couldn't access that kind of ability again by choice.

"Well, I'll just have to come with you as much as I can then. I will, at some point, see what's happening, and I am due to be re-rostered anyway. Hannah can take over here while I'm gone. She's popular with the younger crowd anyway." She crinkled her nose and her eyes sparkled as they always did when she spoke of her daughter.

They were close, and Hannah was as talented as her mother in healing. "Fine, if it helps, please come along and observe. I don't think you'll see anything helpful, though. And thanks for telling me how they're doing." He smiled at her, and she patted his arm before turning away.

"Eva." It was Lilah.

"Yes, dear. What is it?"

"I know a woman who would happily take on the children as her own. She helped Dae and me, and I just know she would love the chance to adopt more. And having them away from this war would be best. Could you please ask Dr Stevenson if he can contact me so we can arrange a meeting about it?" She was brisk, business-like, and Peter wondered why she sounded so formal all of a sudden.

Evaliah blinked then agreed to pass on the message before hurrying away.

Peter turned to her as soon as the door closed. "No lies, Lilah, what was that about?"

"Not here. It's not the right time or place, okay?" She got up and left without a backward glance.

P Ryall

He stood there, dumbfounded.

Escape

Chapter 7

Lilah headed for the carpark so she could call her mother and give her the news. Once in her car, she locked the doors and dialled.

"Hello, Kitty. Are you all right, honey?"

"Hey, Mama. I'm okay. Better than that, actually. Don't freak out, but I have news and I want to make sure you get in on this first. So, today Peter saved two children from another world, but they're orphaned, Mama. They've suffered so much and seen too many bad things, been through things that children should never have to endure. So, I asked Dr Stevenson to reach out to you. I said you would adopt them. I *need* you to get these kids into your care, Mama. It's life and death. I'll explain when I get home, but can you get in touch with your contacts and arrange for them to go to you, like we did?"

"Oh wow. Oh gosh... Yes. I'll call Charlie right now and tell him to contact the doctor in charge, and we'll start integrating them. But you owe me an explanation." She said her goodbyes and promised she was about to make the calls, which was a huge relief.

Nobody knew who those kids were, and why they'd be so vital to this war. Except her. She knew it all. It hadn't even really surprised her that they'd come at this moment, though the circumstances were shocking. At some point, she would have to tell Peter, but right now, it was vital her mother knew what was at stake, and why she needed to ensure the children were safe with their kind.

Then she decided that instead of going home, she would sit with Peter for a while. Her father had been trying to catch her as well. She still felt weird about having another parent, but it was also kind of nice.

As she re-locked her car, she saw her cousin Emma looking around her nervously, apparently trying not to be seen. Even though this behaviour had been normal since that fateful day, Lilah could see the strength in her—like a slight shimmer that clung to her body and distorted the air around her.

The others couldn't see it, though, that much was clear. This was another of Lilah's special gifts, seeing power rather than just feeling it. Thinking about it now, that was why Angel had always given her a very chilled feeling: her magix looked different and felt off, jarring. She'd assumed as a child that it was just her bands that had caused the feelings, but now…well, it was clear what had really happened.

Emma was nervous. It seemed like someone was watching her, but even though she kept glancing around her, she couldn't see anyone. She didn't think it was her uncle; he was busy. Mirren knew her secret but had promised to keep it, and Jeff was snooping around the indoor gardens for her. She'd told him earlier that she would be there today, working. It didn't sit well with her to lie to him—she liked him a lot—but if she let herself get close, he might be a target. She'd stood against the five, and they'd let her live. That wasn't a good sign, and she had seen the look on the lead Huntowra's face; he wanted her to suffer for what she'd done.

Escape

It haunted her, and she'd started to train in secret from that day. She wouldn't let them do to her other loved ones what they'd done to her cousin. Her cousin Lilah. Who was here. She wasn't dead. She had, somehow, miraculously survived. So much trauma and agony, and yet, here she was. A small smile played at the corners of her mouth as she remembered the last time they'd played together, and then seeing her in the ballroom.

It had smashed into her like a behemoth on a rampage, and she'd just frozen on the spot. Peter had fainted, and she'd rushed to check on him. He'd looked at her weirdly then uttered her name. *Lilah.* As soon as it was out, she knew. She just knew what he meant, and she'd scanned the room for her. Seeing her on the staircase, wearing a mask that held her own symbol, her green eyes flashing like re and her soft chocolate curls falling loose and wild to her waist had just taken her breath away. Of course, she'd been reluctant to spend time with her for the same reason she kept everyone at arm's length. To keep her safe from what she knew would come. Retribution.

As she was stepping around the corner, she looked over to the carpark and saw Lilah looking at her with a curious expression. She smiled and lifted her hand in a wave. Emma sighed. She would have to go say hello now. Changing direction, she headed for her cousin.

"Good morning, Lilah." She frowned, noting the formality in her words.

"Hey. Just so you know, I know. And don't worry, I won't say anything to the others. But I might need some help soon, and you're the only one I trust fully to do it." She gave Emma a look that said she meant it.

How the hell could she know? She couldn't. Surely, she meant something else. Emma needed to get her to talk more about *it,* so she didn't slip up. Just as the thought ran through her mind, Lilah's eyes sparkled.

"You won't slip up. I know about the armour, the training...all of it, Em." She said it kindly, but Emma reeled back.

She'd known her thoughts. What did that mean? How was it possible? She looked at her cousin and straight away knew she'd heard those questions too. She blushed bright red but didn't say anything. Apparently, she didn't need to anyway, so what was the point?

Lilah sighed, and Emma remembered then that she'd said she needed her help.

"What do you need my help for?"

"I need to travel soon, and I'll need you to come with me. I remember that day now, clearly. Your armour was already stronger than any of the warriors we had. In fact, I believe you're as powerful as the Aggaron warriors. I want you on my team, when it comes time to select it. We have some time till then, but I'm asking now out of courtesy. But if you say no, I'll insist on it, and it will be ordered by...well, my dad." She rolled her eyes and gave Emma a huge smile.

She had no choice, but honestly, Emma wouldn't let her go without her.

"Yay, that's a yes!"

"Oh my god, stop that. Reading my mind is cheating." After a moment, they both laughed at how childish that sounded.

Escape

"Okay, I'll join this team when it's formed. But until then, just let me keep my armour to myself."

"Sure, that's ne by me. But when you do don it again, there'll be a slight alteration." She grabbed Emma's forearm, and a hot wave shot up in into her chest. "So, everyone knows you're my lieutenant. And it's a power boost. It's something I can do." She held a finger to her lips like she wanted it to stay a secret, though she smiled as she did, and turned back to the main entrance.

Emma stared at her, dumbfounded. She could do that? As she gathered her thoughts, she left. It was getting late, and she needed to start her training.

* * *

Lilah was setting the pieces in motion, gathering the ones she knew were needed. This war was much closer than anyone else realised. She would make sure they were as ready as they could be. She also knew that Peter was about to be made the general for this war, and he would be busy preparing his own army, so she would train her small squad with Dale, and the Great Ones.

Selling the tale to her dad was easy. She said she was taking a pilgrimage and gathering intel, and he approved her request. When they got to the Qualterra, they would sneak off so they could start. She'd already reached out to Mierden telepathically, and he had prepared.

The next step was to get Amara cleared to be a member of her team. That wouldn't be hard since she was a linguistics expert and history buff. The formal request had been lodged already, and she'd spoken with Amara about it. They would have their holiday next week and then, shortly after they returned, set out on this more important journey.

Her mother and brother were getting their people ready here. They knew she was up to something important, but she refused to tell them, other than it was urgent and she would be safe. They had argued with her, but in the end, they admitted it wasn't something they could stop her from doing—she was an adult, after all. Peter had been harder to mollify. He hated being apart from her, and she felt the same way. She wanted to stay with him, even though she knew this was life and death stuff.

As she wandered the halls, thinking absently of all the things she still needed to arrange, there was a loud commotion from the main meeting room, some explosions, a bloodcurdling scream…and then nothing. The air was electric, like the threat of lightning that made your hair stand on end, and she rushed towards the room without thinking. She shoved the door open and ran in then skidded to a halt, staring in horror. A body. There was a body on the floor, mangled and clearly lifeless. She went numb, and her mouth filled with saliva. Bile rose in her throat.

She twisted to the nearby wastepaper bin, only just making it in time. Oh god. Who was it? She was too scared to look. She wanted to just curl into a ball and rock herself until she didn't see it anymore. Didn't smell it. Death, and blood. The whole room reeked of it. The next thing she knew, everything was yelling and chaos. She refused to look again. Tears streamed down her face, and she was drenched in cold sweat.

An agonised cry broke into her mind, a mental scream of anguish. *"Jess, no. Oh hell. Jess."*

The anguish was Ethan's. She wanted to scream, but she was frozen, and her voice seemed to have left her. She just sat

Escape

there, shaking. She rocked and cried harder than ever. Jess. Her family. It couldn't be; she was too…alive. No, this was a mistake. She dared a look then, not at Jess but at Ethan.

He was crouched low near her head, stroking her blood-soaked hair and whispering to her. The words were incoherent; perhaps they weren't even words at all. He was transfixed, looking only at her, grieving too deeply to care what was happening around him. His thoughts were no more than blurred colours and a hissing that should be sound. His pain threatened to crush her.

Peter arrived and hauled his twin up into a tight hug, and Ethan finally broke. Tears started to ow. He tried desperately to hold them off but the harder he tried, the more they came. Seconds later, his legs went out from under him, and Peter was left to support all his weight as he hung limp in his brother's arms. Others quietly placed a sheet over Jess, and moving as one, they gathered her up. Ethan was beyond thoughts now—there was nothing in his mind that made sense—but his agony coated Lilah's mouth like bitter ash. She stared at the brothers, refusing to look at the spot where moments ago a person had been.

The next few days were hectic. Everyone was still in shock, but now there was also anger. Somehow, the two Huntowra prisoners had escaped their cells. Nobody was sure how it had happened, but they'd ripped the cell doors off their hinges, attacked the guards then headed straight for the meeting room, the only place to safely open portals. The trackers had traced them, using magix from their residue, to a barren world. It looked as though they'd been fighting each other. There were signs of it everywhere.

P Ryall

It was odd that they'd even managed to work together long enough to escape. The queens hated their subordinates. Even the elite five were treated poorly, though less than others. This queen had caused the Huntowra they'd captured to practically shrink in terror. He'd all but soiled himself when he realised who she was. It put everyone on edge to know a single queen had this much power, and that she was also patient and manipulative enough to carry out a plan. That went against everything they knew about the species, which they'd always seen as unthinking and spontaneous.

With this new intel, the leaders gathered to change their tactics, while the healers and others ran about getting things ready for the funeral. It was to be held here on Earth so that they were safer, but after Meakra was secured, they would go there with Jess's remains and give her a proper goodbye. Peter had gone to Meakra with some of his brothers to help speed up the repairs. Everyone had things to do, and they buried themselves in it so they didn't have to really feel the loss. They had known other losses, innumerable beings had been snatched away over the years, yet this was harder. They'd begun to feel safe here, to let their guard down and actually have hope that, somehow, this would all work out.

Now, in a week they would bury another royal, hunt the Huntowra, rebuild their homes, and start to finally move back to their worlds, where they at least had access to magix. Of course, moving back was a process, and until this war was decided, there was always danger. Most would stay here until it was safer, but the warriors would be moving on sooner. They would act as a guard, attacking their enemy wherever they could.

Escape

If the death of Jess had done anything, it was that they all wanted to fight now. It would happen, and not everyone would survive it.

Chapter 8

Even though Lilah and Amara had rescheduled their return home to attend Jess's funeral, this trip was to focus on Amara and the memories or dreams she was struggling with. It wasn't unheard of for some people to remember past lives, but this seemed like significantly more. She actually believed that Amara had been trapped somewhere out of time. Amara hadn't aged in all the years they'd been friends. She'd remained exactly the same. Exactly. Which meant that whatever happened to her had infused her with magix. Even if it was only that one gift, she was now more than human.

Lilah was taking her to explore a place she'd recognised from Amara's recollections. She wanted to see just how far out of time her friend really was. Naples, Italy was the only place that t her descriptions, but it was much further out of time than Lilah had ever heard was possible. If that were true, Amara would need significant help adjusting and exploring her new abilities, which couldn't be done here.

What Amara needed was access to a magix ring, experienced healers who could ease her transition, and support from those who would understand what was happening to her. Because if Lilah was right, her friend was about to start exhibiting magix abilities.

Lilah made pancakes for breakfast, letting Amara have a relaxing shower. She was serving her own breakfast when

Escape

Amara came in, dressed in a cool, owing dress and sandals. Her hair had been braided in one single braid, and she wore no makeup. It made her look somehow more innocent, and Lilah smiled at her.

"Morning. Did you sleep well?" She kept her tone light.

"Actually, no. I was having the dreams again, but they seem to be worse now. Everything here feels so right, but also off. It's like I know this place, but I don't. It's different somehow, you know?" She shrugged while reaching for the coffee.

"I arranged for us to come here because I think it's where you were from before."

"What? Why? Kitty, that's not what we agreed to. You better have a damn good explanation."

"I think that you were somehow trapped outside time. It would take a great amount of magix to do that, especially here where it's so limited. But if I am right, Amara, your family may not be here now. They may have died a long time ago."

"That's insane, Kitty. Why would anyone take me out of time or whatever? I'm a nobody." She flashed Lilah a stern look, chewing a pancake as she did. "And why does it matter anyway?"

"Because if you have been taken out of time, and I really think you have, then you've been infused with magix, Amara. You'll need help to understand what's happened and what will happen. Whatever gifts you have will start to show soon enough, and when they do, you need to be in a safe place where the magix can't destroy you as you learn to control it. In many ways, you're like a forbidden one. The power can be too much to handle at first." She looked away, heart heavy.

P Ryall

She didn't want to compare her friend to a forbidden one, but she needed her to understand the danger of not knowing. Lilah had told her all about the forbidden ones as soon as she'd remembered.

Amara looked at her seriously now and chewed her bottom lip thoughtfully before simply nodding and changing the subject. They chatted then about what today's adventure would be, and they made plans to take a picnic basket with them so they could enjoy the whole day without leaving to eat. They would find somewhere to take in the views while watching the excavations happening in Pompeii.

They'd been in the ruins of Pompeii for about two hours when they turned up what had been a busy street, and Amara froze. She knew this.

The road here went up nearly a kilometre then veered slightly to the right before straightening again a mistake from when the roads were laid. Instead of ripping up the area to straighten it, the officials had insisted the workers continue. There had been little time to get this section of road built before wealthy merchants arrived at their new holiday homes. They came from all over to get away from their frantic lives. Some of the elderly moved here for the climate, which was warmer by far than their previous homes.

She wandered these streets lined with eateries, whose smells wafted throughout the city, and brothels adorned with brightly coloured cloths trading food and cloth from her family home just outside the city. She spent endless hours there, watching the city life from her garden, seated under the olive tree with stitching or sketching to help pass the hours.

75

Escape

Amara snapped out of her daydream, dropping her water bottle as she stared at the crumbling streets around her. She took off for her apartment, taking a left at the crooked street, then wove through the rubble some until she reached it. *Home.* There was nothing but bare walls and some pottery, jars that had held oils and jam. She turned to Lilah with tears, finally understanding the truth: she *was* out of time. Two thousand years.

At that moment, the rest fell into place. Hades. He'd done this to hurt Aurelia. Her sweetest, best friend. And a goddess. She had risen against the gods themselves, determined to free them all, and this had been her punishment— after destroying the city that had attempted to hide his sister, Hades had removed her friend from time.

The tears owed freely now, as she stood in the ancient ruins of her home.

"Oh god, Lilah. You're right. I am out of time."

"It's okay, Amara, you aren't alone. You have people who can help you through this. My father has already agreed that you will come with us to Meakra, but I want to take you somewhere else as well. A place we can learn about our magix together." She gave her a sincere smile that was somehow mischievous, and Amara smiled a watery grin back.

* * *

After that, they wandered the streets of ancient Pompeii, and Amara told stories from back when it was the crown jewel of the empire. Lilah was stunned. She'd thrived on history, but this…this was next level. To speak to someone who'd been there…wow.

P Ryall

They made their way to the outer limits of the city and stopped when they reached Amara's family home. The olive tree was still there, and still fruited. They sat there, on the picnic rug under the ancient tree and looked out over what was left of the grand city. It was hard for Lilah to imagine it, but she caught glimpses in her friend's mind, and it made her wish she could have seen it in its heyday.

The rest of their trip was just digging through the rubble. They were told they could keep one small memento, after they signed disclosure forms and agreed never to sell it. It probably had something to do with her being royalty as it surely wasn't normal practice to give priceless artifacts out. She chose a case of scented oil from Amara's home, and Amara chose a statuette of herself and Aurelia. The archaeologist had nervously laughed at how similar she looked to the statue.

Amara murmured, "I'm a relative of theirs. A descendent," as she gently placed the pristine statue in bubble wrap before tucking it into her backpack.

Lilah smiled to herself at that; she wasn't lying.

They spent the last day of their shortened trip just shopping in the small city, buying local garments and jewellery, which according to Amara, were much as they'd been in her time, though the quality was significantly worse. At least Pompeii had genuine precious stones, real gold and silver, and of course, handwoven and dyed fabrics. They stuffed their bags to the brim and made it to the airport in time to have a coffee before their flight back to reality. Neither wanted to really leave, though. Amara because she'd finally started to come to terms with the fact that she would never see her loved ones again, and possibly that Hades, God of the Underworld, had caused the eruption that changed history for all the people of Earth. Lilah

Escape

was just intrigued by the mysteries of life, and the fact that she hadn't really found out more about the ancient ones who'd acted as gods here.

Amara had filled her in on as much as she knew, and they'd gathered written accounts of the local legends as well as history books to take home. Some were not to be found anywhere else in the world, and Lilah was ecstatic with her rare texts.

* * *

Seth greeted the two friends at the airport. He hadn't known Jess, so he was happy to help and get out of the way of grieving people. He never really knew how to act when someone was sad; nobody had taught him the skills. It was a relief that they were both smiling and acting normal...well, as normal as they could, given the situation.

He knew why Lilah had taken her friend away—Jeff had heard it from Peter, who'd repeated it to the emperor. He thought it was cool. Though it would suck, being dragged out of her own time. She might not have felt any pain, but he sympathised with her if she had.

His experience at the hands of that monster had shown him how horrific it could really be out there in the universe. He wanted her to know he was here if it helped in any way, but he didn't want to be pushy either. Bringing dinner to them, offering lifts, these were ne, but there was a line he wasn't prepared to cross. He felt no romance toward either of them and didn't want them to misunderstand his motives.

"Hey, you two. Everyone is...ah, mourning and getting stuff ready, so I volunteered to come get you. Hope that's okay. I don't really do sad crowds all that well." He ushed.

"Oh my gosh, Seth, you'll never guess. She remembers! Pompeii was her home." Lilah's eyes lit so bright they made the sun seem dull.

"Erm, okay... Wait... *What?* Seriously? Pompeii, *the* Pompeii?" he stammered and then covered his mouth. He'd gotten a little loud. "Oops, sorry," he said, more quietly. Wow, that was a shocker. He glanced at Amara, but she didn't seem sad like he'd thought she would be.

"Congrat...ulations?" he half-said, half-asked, not sure what to make of it. Dammit, this was as bad as the sad people stuff back at headquarters. Oh well, at least there wasn't crying here.

"It's okay, Seth, I'm kind of over the shock. Lilah says she can help me with the adjustments, and you know, learning about what magix I'll develop. Guess it could be worse." She smiled and shrugged, but it seemed off to him.

He gave her a considering look then nodded. Deciding to just go with it, he helped the women load their suitcases then he set off for A.S.U. so they could get ready for the next journey. After the funeral.

Escape

Chapter 9

MEAKRA

The morning of the funeral was grey. Everyone was quiet— it was tradition that nobody spoke until after the rites had been said, but even so, the silence seemed bone deep. There weren't words to express that kind of pain, and even if there had been, they would've done nothing at all to help. Peter had stayed with Ethan and helped him get ready even though it brought back the memories of Lilah being declared dead, and the agony.

He tied the traditional warrior scarf around Ethan's neck then adjusted his uniform. He'd decided to honour Jess as a warrior. This was rare; the Talgra took their warrior duties seriously, as seriously as the Aggaron had. It was a true testament to how he felt about her to show her this level of respect. Peter decided then that he too would honour her this way, and he donned his own warrior uniform, in full. Ethan gave him a thankful and somewhat shocked look, and together they made their way to the chapel for the service.

It was packed, lined with guards of honour, and several of their friends had also donned warrior uniforms. Clearly, they weren't the only ones to feel that Jess deserved this recognition. He steered his brother up the aisle to the front. They would be seated with the royal family today, between Matthew and Luca, Jess's father. Ethan stared at the floor as the service started and hummed numbly when the songs of their people were sung in farewell. Towards the end, Lilah stood up and walked to the front, where the coffin was. Not knowing what was happening here, Peter elbowed his brother in the ribs, and he looked up, curious for the first time today.

* * *

"I'm sorry. I know that the custom of our people is silence during a service, but here on Earth, there's a custom I've witnessed called a eulogy. Would it be okay if I perform this custom for Jess today? It's an honour on this world to say things about the departed. To say goodbye." She looked straight at her uncle Luca, and he nodded once.

She then looked at her father, and he frowned but also nodded. Her gaze settled on Ethan; he blinked and smiled. So, she took a deep breath and folded her hands gently in front of her. She looked at all the faces in the room in turn, taking them all in.

"Jessicila, Jess, was one of the strongest women I've ever known. As a child, she was wilful, wild, and just so incredibly blunt. These were qualities that frustrated some, but endeared her to all of us. I wish I'd known her growing up. My own childhood was quite unorthodox, and at times very lonely. When I first saw her as an adult, I didn't even know who she was, but she struck me as a woman who was determined, passionate, and fiercely protective of those she loved. She was quite unimpressed with me, and I honestly didn't know why at the time, but I do know it wasn't personal. I was a new person, someone who'd just showed up and turned the whole world on its head in her mind, and she was worried it would be dangerous for all of you.

Escape

"She reached out to me after my accident, and we had a lunch together. She was sweet, loving, and so very deeply committed to each and every one of you—those who are here, and those who aren't. She told me she would fight with everything in her to make the universe a safe place again, for all of us. She said her dream was to go home and put right all the horrors that had happened. She also said that my death as a child had forever shaped the way our people would fight. There were more warriors than ever now, who wanted vengeance and to stand up to the monsters that had caused all this suffering.

"I want to do right by her. I want to fight as well. Not because my cousin was taken from us, and not because of some dumb prophecy. I want to fight because it's the right thing to do, and we need all of us in this war if we are to stand a chance of stopping the Huntowra. Jess knew that.

"But I can't fight for vengeance. That would make me as guilty as the Huntowra of mindless killing. Jess wanted to fight this war for the right reasons, not for herself. There wasn't even one time she spoke about her own wants, only that she wanted what was best for us all. I'm heartbroken that I didn't get the chance to know her better, or for longer, but I am glad I knew her at all. This universe will be a much darker place without her in it, but I will do what I can to ensure her memory is honoured and that she is never forgotten.

"Please, if you have any fond memories of her, come stand here and share them with us. We may have lost a beautiful soul, but we can choose to celebrate her life with happy memories." She looked again at each of them.

After some unsure glances, she sighed, not sure if she'd just offended everyone, when Luca stood and walked to the front. After that, several others followed, and by the time the service ended, they all wore smiles, even though there was still sadness.

Ethan found Lilah with Peter and Amara after the feast later that day. He seemed unsure, but his voice rang clear as he spoke. "Thank you. I know it was really hard to stand there and say all that stuff. I appreciate it. Though declaring you're gonna fight this war was a bit touchy. Most of us want to wrap you in bubble wrap and keep you safe. I know Peter here was about to flip his lid when you announced that. Your dad also seemed pretty mad about it."

"Yeah, well, they can get over it. I survived this long, and I know that to win this, we all have to fight it. There isn't any way around that fact, even for my dad. Don't worry, I have a feeling we aren't in it alone, though." She winked at him then changed the subject. "Oh hey, not sure if you remember, but this is my friend Amara. I was just saying to her that when we leave here, she won't need to bring anything with her. She was going to try bring everything. Of course, she should bring a few knickknacks, but you know, nothing like clothes and stuff." She eyed Amara then rolled her eyes, looking at Ethan.

* * *

He smiled automatically and held his hands up, backing away. "Argh. Secret women's talk. Sorry I interrupted." He grinned hugely at Amara, who looked as though she might slap him.

For some reason, that was funny to him, and he left feeling really confused by it. Jeff found him a short time later, sulking in a corner, but as usual he didn't even say anything, just stayed near him. He wished sometimes that he could feel other's feelings as well, but then he was glad not to when he thought of

Escape

days like this. How hard must it be to have all your own sorrow and the grief of entire worlds on top of it? Was that why Jeff was so silent? How would it be to live in his head? He didn't ask; that would just be rude and honestly, he didn't know that he really wanted to hear the answer.

Jeff grimaced every now and then—was it a pain reaction?—but they watched silently as the room around them clamoured to life. People told stories of Jess, some funny and some downright scary. Lilah's little Earth ritual seemed to bring them all closer together, sharing happiness for Jess instead of just pain and sorrow. It did help. He wasn't feeling as isolated and empty as he had been.

He glanced over to where she was standing now, chatting to her friend, and his left arm started twitching. The sensation quickly built to a burn, and he swallowed convulsively. He didn't want this, not now. There was no way he would offer his hand to anyone. Jess wasn't even properly mourned yet, and despite never being bound to her, he loved her deeply enough to want time to mourn her absence. Why the hell was this happening? Why now, and why him? It wasn't fair. He wanted to scream and shout and break things like a child. Which was only natural—anyone who'd just lost someone would hate the idea that there was a perfect t for them so suddenly.

He'd met her before, of course. But that had been in the mortal world—hers—and naturally his hand hadn't twitched or burned him at all. The limited magix on Earth stopped that. But now they were near a magix ring, his hand might just bloody explode into flames any minute.

He practically growled at Jeff, "S'cuse me a minute," and stomped off.

He let himself out the front doors, walking past a corridor of arched windows and round to the garden hidden beside the building. The light here was dim, but he noticed two people trying not to be seen. They were across the fountain, sitting close and chatting quietly. The one on the left seemed angry about something, and the one on the right was desperately trying to say something—her hands were uttering in front of her, and she looked worried. Were they having a lover's tiff or was this something more?

It was odd that life was still happening in front of him. It should've stopped for them all. He felt like he'd been ripped out of the world and was looking at it from a glass box that nobody else could see, hidden and lonely and screaming in agony all at once. After a few minutes, he couldn't stand it anymore, and he went back indoors. Instead of heading for his dorm, he sat near the Starling Trumpets, letting the soothing sensation take hold of him. It was nice to feel soothed for even a minute.

"Did the wake get too much for you?" Amara was there as though he'd conjured her unconsciously, and he was instantly annoyed because she could take away the pain, and he didn't even know her yet.

"Pretty much. I seem to be over a lot of things right now, actually." He didn't even look in her direction, just shrugged and stared ahead.

"Me too. I know it's not polite, but this is kind of a wake for my family as well. I can't bury them, though. That ship sailed a really long time ago." She sighed and sat heavily on the cool stone next to him.

Now he was curious. *Shit*.

Escape

"Your family needs a wake?" He didn't even care if the question was rude.

"Yeah, they're all dead and turned to dust. I was thinking on the plane that it would be nice to have someone, anyone, who was my family, right now. Apart from Lilah and Dae, of course. But, biologically, it's just me now. I'm suddenly here, and I don't know why nobody can see that I want to scream and chuck stuff. They're completely oblivious to my suffering, except for Lilah. She's always seen things differently. I can't help but wonder if that's part of her gift." She rubbed her head anxiously.

He couldn't help but ask, "What are you doing? Is your forehead itching?"

"Huh? Oh. No, it's ne." She ushed. "Just checking for new bits. Apparently, I was infused with magix, somehow, and I'll get new abilities. I'm kinda terrified about it all, actually." She was fidgeting with her arms and rocking slightly.

Why did she have to be...perfect?

He wasn't getting away from her; he saw it already. There would come a time where he would offer her his hand, and they would be bound. He loathed the idea right now, but even just these few minutes with her had shown him that she was exactly right for him. The Talgra knew when it was the right one; this had been the way their world worked for as long as anyone knew. Jess would've hated it. He snorted without thinking about it.

She looked at him, wounded, and he rushed to explain. "Oh, sorry. That wasn't meant for you. I was thinking about Jess and her reaction to something, and it was just... I'm sorry," he finished lamely.

P Ryall

She sat silently for a minute, and then Lilah came out looking for her. "Oh, Amara, there you are—" She saw Ethan and stopped. "I can come back, if that's better." She was teasing, but neither of them laughed.

She shrugged, turned, and left them to it.

They sat there in silence for what seemed like forever, but eventually the wake ended, and the guests started to leave.

It was time to say goodbye, but it was oddly hard. "Well, guess I'll head off now…"

"Yeah, uh, my family's probably looking for me. I should…"

They laughed at each other.

With a last look at her, Ethan turned and went through the doors again.

* * *

Only when the door shut did she turn and ee the building. She needed to cry. She wasn't even sure why. She sent a quick message to Lilah, letting her know she was on her way home already then, she switched off her phone. She needed to start really processing what had happened to her and her family, and she didn't want to have to put on a strong front. She wanted to scream and cry and be miserable, just for a while. It was proper, and she was determined to have her own farewell for her loved ones.

This funeral and wake had really given her a lot to think about. She would find a way to say her goodbyes, and then she would move on. Of course, she was also leaving Earth, so she wanted to grieve for them, and for all those lost in that horrific

Escape

event. Perhaps learning about who she was and the monster who'd stolen her world from her would help heal her heart.

She skipped dinner, not feeling hunger after such a tumultuous few weeks.

Chapter 10

Dragons didn't understand death the way other species did —for them, it wasn't the end. The amount of energy released by a dragon's death was enough to carve out new rivers and could often be felt lingering. Their bodies decayed, but it was commonly accepted that their energy lived on. Mirren tried to express sadness for Jess, but she wasn't really gone. He, and the other dragons attuned to even the smallest energies, felt hers still.

Ethan didn't like that, and they argued over it endlessly in the days following the funeral. He wasn't ready to talk about losing her. In all honesty, he might never be ready, but Mirren suggesting that she was still present really angered him. He'd refused to join the scout Mirren was on, even though he'd been selected for it. Instead, he'd swapped with a human whose name he didn't even know yet.

He was now searching the lesser-known Qualterra ravines. They'd only been discovered a year ago, and it looked like there were several tube-like caves littering them. It was the last place anyone would look for rogue Huntowra.

His determination to get to them before they could be apprehended was his driving force. He didn't want them caught; he wanted them dead. No second chances. They should've been executed the second they were captured, but the others wanted intel. Numbers, gathering worlds, victims they'd recently

Escape

targeted...the list was endless. But the Huntowra were nothing but brutality, their one goal to destroy and murder. He was done with them. He would kill them on sight.

It was an inevitable part of war, one his people had yet to understand. To win this, they would lose their empathy. They had to. Otherwise, killing even the Huntowra would eat away at their consciences.

He would start his hunt here, tracking until he found the monsters. He wanted them to see his face as they died and know that this was vengeance for her. He was wandering the edges of the ravines, ignoring the chatter from his fellow scouts. Their tone was sombre. Jess's death had at least impressed on the majority how cruel and brutal this war really would be, but they joked still—light-hearted banter meant to ease their fears.

"Shut up. The last thing I wanna hear now is jokes about slugs." He glared at them.

Jack looked taken aback. "Sheesh, Ethan, get over yourself. We all lose people. It's a fact of life. You can't just—"

"Jack, you're being an idiot. He's a Talgra. They don't actually lose that many of their people. Just goes to show how emotionally stunted they are." It was said in a whisper, but he caught it anyway.

"Oh right...*sorry*," he said louder.

He would be if he kept going. Ethan scowled and turned away from them again, deciding to focus on where he was going. After that, the others did try to keep their chatting quieter, but it may as well have been yelling. He—and the Huntowra, for that matter—could hear it all.

Legend said that the Talgra were descended from an ancient canine species, and that was still evident in their lives today. They called their young 'pups' and multiple pregnancies were common, just like litters. After doing some research on Earth, he was convinced that his ancestor species was similar to wolves, although significantly larger. Earlier histories of Earth described something that seemed to resemble the actual Talgra wolf species: the humans had called them moon children, or werewolves. He'd delved into some of those histories, trying to learn more. Curiosity was his weakness, and he was tempted to ask Lilah for some help with it. He wasn't sure if Peter would be upset about it, so he would ask him to join in on the project. If they won the war. And they survived it. And he was still curious.

He was growing more and more frustrated, wanting his armour. Battle. He wound his way deeper into the Qualterra, but after endless walking, decided that it was time to check out the interior of the caves. Just then, a faint stench of a rotting carcass reached his nose. The Shrogan wouldn't have left it. He held his hand up in a closed fist, signalling the others to halt. They immediately went quiet and stopped in their tracks, waiting for Ethan to give an order. Their glances around were alert and nervous but determined—how incredibly brave this species was. He made his way round another bend and saw a large, cow-like beast, mangled. It was done unmistakably by a Huntowra.

"Stay alert. There's a Huntowra near," he radioed his team.

"Roger that, boss. We'll spread out and scan the landscape. Radio check-ins every five minutes, guys."

There were a few assents before his earpiece went silent.

Escape

While his team went off to climb the cliffs, getting a bird's eye view of the scene, he checked the carcass for clues. How many had been here? How long ago? Were there any footprints he could use to track them? He knelt at the beast's side. The blood here was still warm and sticky. It hadn't even started to clot yet; this was a very fresh kill. The smell was awful, though every creature smelled like that when they were gutted. Large chunks of flesh had been ripped away from the beast's body without severing any of the main blood vessels. What a shit way to die.

He was intently scanning some footprints when his radio squealed into life. "Fuckers sneaking up on you, Connor. Watch your six," Jack warned.

A few seconds later gun re erupted. There was screeching from an angry Huntowra and then it faded, leaving an echo.

"He's headed underground, fellas," Connor said calmly. "Let's go hunting."

"Okey-dokey, boys, let's go get this oversized turkey and stuff it with lead." Jack was nearly laughing, clearly thinking he was funny.

Ethan followed, nodding to Jack, who was only a few meters from him now, and they each took separate caves. It was dark enough to need their torches, but at least the air was much cooler than outside. They stayed in touch with the radios, which were a little scratchy because of all the rock.

Ethan stopped for a minute and used his magix. "Can you guys hear better now? I boosted the radios. Try to keep talking to a minimum, though. They can hear better than dogs."

Several assents came over his radio, but he didn't know who was whom. It didn't matter. They had heard.

He was surprised how deep the caves went and was just about to turn around when the tunnel opened into a much bigger cavern. It was easily the size of the main meeting room back at headquarters and had stalagmites that glowed in neon colours. Pinpricks of light from other tunnels told him his team were just catching up to him.

"Whoa," someone murmured over the radio.

None of them had expected this to exist in a dump like Qualterra. Even he was shocked by it.

The electric feeling of Huntowra magix hung in the air—they had created a portal. His shoulders slumped.

"They're gone. Someone get in touch with headquarters and give them our position. They'll have to send the trackers in." He crouched and took a minute.

Dammit. He hated this cat and mouse game. Why couldn't they just outright attack, already? These sneak attacks were annoying.

He listened as the others chatted. It didn't bother him now; they weren't scaring off any beasts. They waited for about two hours before they heard talking and footsteps. When he looked up, Hogan and Bryant were walking towards them, serious and conversing in low tones. Hmm, that was interesting. His brother had been avoiding his tracker instincts for as long as he could remember. Why was he suddenly here now?

***

They set to work without talking to anyone. Bryant hadn't wanted to do this, but the bitch he'd caught and her

Escape

follower had killed his brother's love. He owed them payback, so here he was. This wouldn't take long. Hell, the only reason Hogan was here was because he needed someone to stabilise the edges of the reverse portal. If he could've figured out how to do that on his own, he wouldn't have asked him to come along. Now Hogan was all excited, thinking Bryant had come to his senses and was joining his team. He had the greatest respect for them, but he wasn't about to join. He wasn't going to sit around *teaching* when he could be out there *helping*. It seemed fundamentally wrong to teach children how to do this when he already could. If they hadn't been at war, sure, but not now. Not like this. They needed every hand, and he was great with a sword as well thanks to his brothers.

They had taught him over the years, despite him not being a warrior. His older brothers, in particular, were incredible with combat, though he didn't know if his baby brother had been holding out on that as well. Peter had shocked everyone with his secret. He'd hidden it basically his entire life, which was scary and meant that he'd have hidden any abilities that could accidently give him away as well.

He heard Hogan's incantations and focused. He didn't really need to, but he wanted to be safe, and that required him to do the right things. They worked quickly to open the portal and identify the world.

It was an older one that had been abandoned a couple of thousand years ago by a cannibalistic lizard-like species, the Crowoals. Their planet had been decimated by a meteor shower, only the meteors were the size of buildings and the shower had lasted a decade. The survivors had scattered across the universe, but they still existed in parts that were remote and heavily forested. Mostly they ate raw meat like behemoths, but they also still practised ritual cannibalism. The terrain on this world would be hard. His brother would've usually avoided a world like this, but judging by the gleam in his eyes, he was going, regardless. He sighed, not wanting to be the one to tell their parents.

"Be careful. Come home safe and well, brother," he murmured and then left.

He didn't want the response his brother muttered, and he didn't stop to watch him and his team go either. He had more to do here before he returned home.

* * *

Ethan and his team went into the thick forest, careful not to fall and watching for wildlife. There weren't any bird-like creatures, but there were snakes—exceptionally large ones that made the anacondas on earth look like worms. Several other apex predators hunted here as well, some feline but others like nothing the humans had seen before. There was a large equine-type creature that was strictly a meat-eating animal. They had three sets of razor teeth, each one an inch in length, and their legs were like tree trunks. They used their clawed feet to incapacitate prey and had a screech that shattered glass and caused the land to slide in unstable areas.

This world was as hard for Etan's team as the caves had been for the Huntowra, and he brie y wondered why they'd gone to the trouble of hiding when heading straight to their worlds was clearly a safer choice. What were they searching for? And why go out of their way to prevent even their own kind from following them? It wasn't making sense.

The trees here grew out of old buildings and ground litter built up in areas that had once been clear for the civilization that had been here. The problem with that was that the ground was

Escape

often unstable and had significant drops, as much of it was in fact the tops of old buildings and temples.

The team trod carefully. Conner slipped a few times, swearing. "Sorry, boss-man, I didn't know the terrain would be so shit. I'm pretty bad at hiking and stuff." He sounded embarrassed.

"Don't worry. The trees here will muffle the sounds somewhat, just keep being careful. Jack, I want you to take the rear and let Conner be mid. That way, if he slips, we have a better chance of stopping him from falling into an old ruin."

He'd at-out lied about the trees, but it didn't really matter that they would be heard. With all the other wildlife moving about, the Huntowra wouldn't worry about stray people. What *was* a problem was that the dense foliage meant it was hard to find a trail they could follow. He eventually found one, though, and they stopped frequently to check they were still on the right path. Conner seemed happy about that. It gave him the chance to breathe and feel steadier.

They were winding downwards. The trees seemed to grow ever larger, and the ruins were more visible at this level. Just before nightfall, they reached a at area, the flooring of an old temple, and they set up camp. Ethan raised protective barriers and muffled them from being heard, and Jack wrangled the others to set up swags and gather water from a nearby stream. They had a gas cooker and ready to eat meals and sat there talking happily until they were finally tired enough to sleep.

Except for Ethan. He sat there with his thoughts and memories, trying to imagine what Jess would have done in this place. She hated forests but loved them at the same time. She had been a complete contradiction; it was why he'd loved her so much. She would've slapped him for bringing her here, and he would've laughed that she thought it would hurt his feelings. She was such a brat but so loyal, and he hurt from missing her. It was a physical pain like someone had reached into his chest and was squeezing his heart, while also breaking his bones, repeatedly, and he couldn't even pass out from the pain of it.

He was sitting there picturing her, missing her, when a scream came from the direction of the stream. It wasn't his people—they'd all come running with loaded guns. Had some other human population decided to come here? It seemed odd that anyone would want too, though. And then it clicked. The Huntowra.

The male had been fearful of the female one, and they'd never learned her identity. Could they be fighting? Was she vicious enough to cause this amount of screaming? He didn't know much about the queens of the Huntowra, only that there were a lot of legends about them being like bees, with the queens at the top of the food chain in the hive. He and the others decided to split up and check it out. If this were a trap, they were about to see first-hand how cunning and savage the Huntowra really were.

The teams separated and went in different directions, taking care not to be heard or seen. They reached the stream at the same time. There was no other wildlife around, and they met in the middle. Jack was scratching his head when another man made a horrible gagging sound, covering his mouth and looking across the riverbank. They all looked over slowly and saw it. A man was strung up against the cliff face. His face was bruised, his body covered in angry, swollen lumps. But that wasn't the worst of it, and there was no mistaking what had done this. It was the same as Seth had suffered. The male was still alive,

Escape

bleeding from where he'd been partially skinned. This wasn't over for him yet.

Ethan wanted to vomit, but he pushed the feeling down. Helping this being was more important than his hunt. They would rescue him and take him to safety. The others agreed, and together they clambered to the man and cut him down. They knew from Seth that this was likely the only chance they would get to save him. The monster would let him partially heal and then come back to finish him. They carefully wrapped him in space blankets then made their way back to the safe area so they could portal out. Everyone was twitchy and constantly looking over their shoulders, but there was nobody following them.

Chapter 11

ARTH

Peter and Damon were in the meeting room when the portal opened. They took one look at Ethan's team and fell silent. They were holding something between them, wrapped in a thermal blanket. Had they killed a Huntowra? Damon was closer to them than Peter, who'd been on the staircase to prune the Starling Trumpets. As he looked at the faces of the team, he heard a rustle. The blanket was moving. *Shit.* Someone was hurt.

He mentally did the math, and all the team were here and safe, so who was this? Peter seemed to realise that then, and he barked an order at his brother before vanishing. Damon didn't even have the time to process before several others appeared and demanded they take the victim to an emergency treatment room. He followed them as if he were in a trance. He needed to know what had happened, because if this was like Seth, then how badly had his sister been hurt by them? He didn't know if anyone knew what she had suffered, only that she had. They'd all been told that she'd merely been thrown from a great height, but was that true? He had doubts.

Damon watched in horror as the healers gently unwrapped the man then promptly vomited into a nearby wastepaper bin. Thick vines bound each limb, constricting his hands and feet, which were bruised and swollen. His face looked

Escape

like he'd been through a cheese grater, and pretty much every part of him was visibly bruised or broken. Was his sister hiding the truth from them all about what had happened to her? He had a hard time believing she'd simply been discarded; she'd always done her best to protect others from seeing her pain and vulnerabilities.

He watched now as the healers tried frantically to save the life of the poor soul in front of them, though he doubted it would be possible. And even if they did, he would never be the same, not mentally. Seth was certainly struggling to move on from his attack, and he had lots of support and therapy to help him.

Damon stood as a sentinel, and was joined over the following hours by Connor, Jack, Riley, and Garret. They had gone to clean up, and they were all shaken. Nobody wanted to say anything…but what could they have said anyway?

Suddenly, in unison, the healers stood back. They were crying, having done all they could for the soul on the table. He was breathing, just, but whether he lived or not would depend on him. The marks and swelling had all but disappeared—as a magix being he could be healed much more than humans, even with the restrictions of Earth.

Damon remembered his last conversation with Evaliah, his mother's mentor. She'd been doing some healing sessions for his sister, and she was exhausted.

"Just a little healing, dear," she'd said to him when he looked like he'd been slapped by her offer. "It would at least help restore the memories of your family. Wouldn't you like that?" She'd been shocked when he'd gotten angry at her.

"I *have* a family, *my* family. I don't want to remember the death of a whole planet. Not remembering is a blessing. I don't have to have the screams or images of horror to keep me awake at night. Instead, I was gifted an amazing mother, a childhood free of war and agony. I had a father who was a role model. And I found my sister, and blood or not, she means the world to me."

Since then, he'd decided to at least use his birth name, though his people called him Dae. That was his preferred name, but he wouldn't tell anyone else that he'd made this choice. They would see it as him accepting his biological father, and he wasn't ready to do that—not yet, at least. He wanted to protect himself and his father from more pain by bonding with him. He also wanted to be more like Troy, a powerful warrior, and his training was coming along well. But his father, his biological one, would want Damon safe and out of the way.

Not happening, he thought savagely, and he focused again on the man fighting for life in front of him.

He didn't realise until everyone else had gone that he was hungry. He jumped as his belly let out an almighty growl. He chuckled to himself, sighed, and then left. He was having dinner at Lottie's tonight. His mother was still teaching the younger group to block attacks, and his sister had been either working or with Peter most of the week.

Damon ate until his belly hurt. He had been hungrier than ever since he started training. They'd worked on his stamina, shielding, and dodging. Now he would learn about attacking and sword wielding. There was also the other thing he was learning: magix control. His mother had given him some concoction that allowed him to access the magix he hadn't known he had. It was exhausting, but he was glad to be learning, finally. Of course, his

Escape

magix, like all their magix, was extremely limited here. He'd been told he needed to build up his tolerance, otherwise he would essentially be no different from the forbidden. That hadn't meant much, not at first. But now he knew and was glad to be grounded to this world. For now, anyway.

He'd also been surprised to learn that there was a whole separate, and very secret, government keeping the Aggaron hidden, even from other humans. He'd met with a few of them. They weren't army types, which was a shock. There were ministers, bankers, mayors, council workers, doctors, and more among the ranks of those who helped hide and integrate the Aggaron into Earth life. They provided everything needed to make an alien look as though they'd always been here, from papers to money, false degrees, and even cars and homes. Their mission was to protect the Aggaron and give them sanctuary until the great war. Theirs was an old religious group that descendants had been handed into as they came of age to continue.

Unlike other religions, this one had factual basis. They aliens lived here, unageing and blessed with gifts not of this world. In exchange for their safe harbour here, the Aggaron helped with technological and even medical advances, though not at a pace that would hurt the natural development of the world. It had happened in the past that the Aggaron had helped a world advance, only to have that world destroy itself. It had left a deep scar in the psyche of all Aggaron, so they had secluded themselves and had strict laws prescribing who they shared their knowledge with.

But even this world was on the edge. They'd reached a critical point in their evolution. Either they would stand up and stop their destruction, or they would die, much sooner than they realised. And that was assuming they all survived the coming war with the Huntowra.

Damon sighed. His mind was so busy tonight. He needed a shower, and sleep. Since he was alone here, he stripped off in the hallway and padded to his small bathroom naked. He adjusted the water temperature and stepped in, letting the hot water rain down on him. He stood there with his eyes closed, letting the water caress his aching muscles. After a while, he shaved and lathered himself with soap. The movements were automatic, but they hurt, every muscle screaming in protest.

After he was done, he snapped the water off and took a deep breath before stepping out and grabbing a towel. He wrapped it around his waist and used another to dry his chest and hair. He was headed for his wardrobe when he noticed he wasn't alone anymore. Seth was sitting on the far end of his bed with his shoulders slumped. He wasn't even looking, but Damon could tell he was upset. How had he gotten in? And when? Damon blinked stupidly.

"Seth?" He approached him slowly. "What's wrong? And no offense, but how the hell did you get in here?"

"Oh, hey, Dae. Sorry, I didn't know where else to go. I didn't wanna be there tonight. That guy, they say it was the same Huntowra that had me." His voice broke as he spoke. "That could have been…no, it would have been me if I hadn't made a run for it. But what if that guy was taken was to replace me? I feel really shit. I don't want Jeff to worry any more than he already is, so I kinda just drove around. I saw you at the lights down the road and decided to call in. You left the front door wide open, by the way. Should be more careful about that. Anybody could wander in, you know?" He shrugged absently, not seeming to realise he'd done just that.

Escape

Damon was speechless. They thought the one responsible for Seth's injuries was the same one who'd caused all that damage? It was worse than he'd thought, because they knew this was one of the Elite Five, who'd abducted his sister as a little girl. How could beasts like this not have caused her more harm? He felt a sudden rage, and the house shook.

Seth blinked, panicking and running for the doorway, shouting, "Earthquake!"

Damon didn't bother. His anger had caused it. He needed to be careful, otherwise he'd need to explain himself to people he didn't want to. Like his father. Matt.

Shit. Breathe, idiot. Don't blow it now.

He took some calming breaths, and the shaking stopped. Seth was still braced in the doorway. He didn't look worried, but there was a glint of curiosity in his expression.

"Hmm, that's weird. We don't generally get quakes here." He shrugged.

It seemed to have distracted him from his melancholy, though, and Damon took advantage of that. He would catch up with him at work, but his exhaustion was really starting to weigh on him.

"Hey, listen, Seth. I gotta get some sleep, but did you wanna hang out sometime? We can go have a beer or something. Maybe get a few of us together. Hell, we can even make it a barbeque or something."

Seth grinned then his face fell a little again. "Thanks. Sorry I barged in. I don't have many Earth friends who know about all this stuff. I mean, there's Travis, of course, but he'll run to Jeff with anything like this. They seem awfully close nowadays. It's nice to see Trav happy, but it makes it hard for me when I have to edit everything I don't want to share with my brother." He blushed and looked down sheepishly, clearly feeling at odds with his thoughts. It didn't seem like he was jealous, but he was coming across as somewhat insecure. Hopefully, he worked through it.

Damon nodded mutely and walked Seth to the front door. They said goodnight, and Damon locked it, turning off lights on his way back upstairs. He was so tired now that he didn't even bother with dressing or pulling back the covers. He simply flopped onto his bed and was snoring. His dreams were scary, but he didn't fully wake until he rolled over and fell onto the floor. He tried to get back to sleep, but it didn't happen, so he dressed and had some breakfast.

Damon walked into the infirmary to check on the patient, and to see if Hannah was able to help him with his sore muscles. Normally, it wouldn't matter who did the healing, but honestly, he liked her lots. Stupidly lots. And besides, Evaliah would ask too many questions and wouldn't be side-tracked. Hannah believed in letting her patients have their own private thoughts, and that was a blessing, all things considered.

He found Hannah and asked if she was able to ease sore muscles.

She nodded thoughtfully and chewed her lip as she indicated for him to sit.

He did as she asked, and she silently got to work on his back. It took him a few minutes to realise she wasn't herself, and he looked at her closely. Her eyes were tight and didn't seem to have the same sparkle in them. She had a downward turn to her generally smiling mouth. Her bluish-tinted skin was duller

Escape

today, which made her appear unwell, and her hair was pulled up severely into a bun. Something was wrong. Was she sick? What had he missed? He stared at her trying to see what else he'd missed when her eyes met his.

She gave him a grim smile and sighed. "Well, that'll do it. Be sure to stay hydrated. You appear to have forgotten that you need water to survive."

"Hey, what's wrong? You seem down. Can I help with anything?"

"No, I'm ne. Just worried, I guess." She shrugged. "You can go now." She turned and walked away.

Wow.

What the hell was that about? He yanked his shirt over his head savagely. Why had she dismissed him so rudely? She was never rude. Ever. He was preoccupied as he made his way to the intensive care unit and was taken aback when he realised the bed was empty. Panic burned in his belly, and he had to concentrate to keep his emotions in check.

"Yeah, I know. I was shocked when I got here too." Seth was leaning against the far wall. Damon hadn't even seen him.

"Did he pass?"

"Nah, they say he woke up early and started screaming. They moved him to a...quieter area with some forest. I think they said he's with the Visper in their habitat." He shrugged and pushed away from the wall. "Catch you later, okay? I'm headed to a meeting with your dad. Wish me luck." He gave Damon a half smile as he left.

"Good luck," Dae whispered to the now-empty room.

Everyone seemed so damned depressed today. What the hell was happening? His phone buzzed, and he hurriedly answered, grateful for the distraction.

It was Ashlyn. His mother had taken to phoning him at strange hours and demanding he attend some new training. He hadn't expected to hear from her yet, though.

"Hey, what's up? You remember I'm at work today, don't you?"

"Of course, but I have this weird feeling. Are you okay? Is your sister okay? I had a quick call from her yesterday to tell me she's taking a trip for a while and not to worry, but all I can do is worry."

He was instantly alert. "Wait, Lilah's going somewhere? Peter isn't, and they generally can't be separated." *Crap.* He'd missed something.

"Yes, she said she has some work stuff planned, and she's taking a full escort with her. Apparently, Peter has some royal duties to attend to here, since you haven't stepped up yet as the heir, so he's doing what you should be doing, as well as his own stuff." She did keep the edge from her voice fairly well, but he heard her disapproval and was instantly defensive. "I don't want to be some pampered prince. I need to help, Mom. Sitting around and staying safe is pointless if there are no people left to rule."

"I know. And I agree. Besides, it's against the nature of Aggaron to stand by and watch. Your mother Amanda, she was a feisty one. My stars, she was so incredibly stubborn and strong-willed... I know from her letters that she and your father often had words about her being a warrior." There was real amusement in her voice, and Damon was left speechless.

Escape

His mom had been a warrior too? He felt a sharp pain in his chest and blinked tears away as he cleared his throat. "Aww, Mom, I didn't know that. Thanks. It's nice to know something about her."

She made a small sound that was both happy and sad. "Okay, well, listen, your sister will be away and definitely safe, so I sent a hospital report from our people to the A.S.U asking for you to have leave, because I sadly had a car wreck and am recovering. And you, my beloved son, are looking after me for a short time. We're taking a trip to the desert, actually, so we can practice some less-common war scenarios. Basically, we're going to an area void of people and hidden from satellites, where we will host the biggest play ever, using our limited magix, and blow stuff up as well. Even try out some new tech we developed, *hopefully*. So, pack a bag, and be shocked when you hear I had a bad accident."

And just like that, she hung up. What was with everyone? Was he the last sane creature here? He shoved the phone in his pocket, not even worried now about getting to his desk. It was only a matter of time before he was sent home anyway. He was standing in the corridor for a few minutes, staring into space, when Emma came across him.

"Oh, hey, Damon. You okay? Looks kinda like you got lost or something." She gave him a friendly smile.

"Yeah, actually, I'm good. Just heard that my sister's going on a trip. There was a time I would've been told first, but I guess now it's all different." He rolled his eyes, but he still sounded bitter.

"Oh, yeah, I know. Actually…I'm one of her guards. Well, sort of. It's complicated. But don't worry, we're going via netherworlds that are protected and we'll be in every shield and protection there is. She'll be perfectly safe." She gave him an affectionate smile and ruffled his hair.

He blinked slowly, processing that.

Huh. And then it dawned on him. They were cousins. He hadn't even acknowledged it before. And more than that, she was *the* cousin, the one who'd tried to stop his sister from being abducted in the first place. A weight lifted off his chest, and he sucked in a sharp breath.

"Aww, shit. I didn't even realise. God, I'm stupid some days. Sorry." He slapped his forehead then felt ridiculous when Emma looked more confused than ever. "Oh, um. I just realised we're cousins. Sorry. I don't remember… Amnesia, you know?" He jabbed a finger at his scar.

She looked at him blankly for a second then laughed out loud. "It's okay. I guess I seemed pretty weird, huh? I forgot you don't remember. Sorry if I offended or upset you just now." She reddened, looking embarrassed.

His face heating, he shuffled his foot and mumbled, "It's okay. I don't mind. It just takes some getting used to. Anyway, I'm taking a trip as well, with my mom. Stay safe, though, and look after her for me, okay?"

She nodded, her eyes serious in an instant.

Just then Caleb bounded over to them. "Hey, you two. Dae, check it out, boss man wants a word. Sounds important." He didn't bother to keep his voice low.

"Boss man?" He was so confused.

"Ah…yep. Your dad, or whatever you call him, I guess."

Escape

"Really. He wants to talk to me?"

Fuck. Was this about him being a prince again? He'd hoped he'd gotten through to his biological father about that. Groaning loudly, he turned and stomped off in the direction of Matt's offices. He wanted to get this over with already. He heard the others behind him as he stomped off.

"Are you set for the trip? Don't forget, tell no one else. We meet at seven AM sharp," Emma hissed at Caleb.

"Hmph, I know. I'm not a total idiot," he grumbled at her.

Damon couldn't make out anymore, he was too far away, but he was curious now. Was Caleb really going with them on their trip? He was surprised. Nobody seemed to like him much; he wouldn't have guessed they were close. He shoved the thoughts aside as he turned the corner and saw Matt standing there, impatiently. His arms were crossed, and he was tapping a foot absently.

Matt looked up and saw Damon. He looked tired—he probably was, but Damon didn't want to see it. He didn't want to feel sad or sorry for his father. What he'd done was the right thing. He was sure of that.

Matt straightened and nodded in greeting.

Damon copied him but kept his jaw clenched. "Caleb said you needed to talk to me"

"I do. And it's not about…you know, you being my heir. It's about your mother." He shifted uncomfortably, and Damon realised what this was about.

"Oh, yeah, that. She called me. She needs me to help her for a bit. Something about an accident. She says she'll be okay, but she's stubborn." He made a tiny popping gesture with his mouth, trying to sound worried and annoyed.

He couldn't pretend to be surprised with this man. He was his father, after all, and had probably seen a lie or two from his children. It would be better if he just kept to the truth as best he could.

His father gave him a sharp look but then shrugged and nodded. "Oh, that's good. That she called, I mean. I hope she makes a full recovery. You've been approved for paid leave. The papers," he withdrew some documents from his jacket pocket, "have all been signed, and if you need further time off, just let us know, okay?" He didn't look directly at his son, and Damon knew this was hard for him.

"Thanks," he mumbled and then he stood there for a minute, in the most awkward silence he'd ever experienced, before deciding on the spot to add, "Hey. When things are more…settled, we should go get a beer or something. You look like you need one."

Matt smiled widely then let out a chortle. "Beer…I need more than a beer, kid." He rubbed his face with the backs of his hands, and Damon smiled. His sister often did that too.

They both grinned, and for a moment, Damon felt a closeness he didn't want but couldn't deny. He said his goodbyes and thanked Matt for delivering the message then left for his mother's.

* * *

"Hey, Mom, sorry it took so long to get here. There was a stupid amount of…*what the fuck?*" Damon blinked.

Escape

His mother was at the kitchen table, her arms bloodied and stuck in some crazy-looking plant that seemed to be chomping away at her. She looked at him calmly and smiled. He was stunned and rushed to try to help her, but she laughed and shook her head at him.

"Don't, it's a Karra pod. They're native to Helios, but we brought a few with us and are cultivating them. They are basically the same as leeches. They clean the blood, but the method is, well, kind of strange. It has my arms but could do the same with legs or even tentacles. We use them for venom bites, and their roots can also be ground and made into a powerful sedative. This might look like a monster movie scene, but I assure you I'm ne. And no, it doesn't hurt."

Damon nodded mutely then turned to the fridge; he needed a drink. But thinking of the plant, he also kinda needed to throw up. What a day this was turning out to be. He offered his mother a beer, but she just shook her head without speaking. Clearly, the blood cleaning was gonna take some time, so he settled himself where he couldn't see the plant of horror and watched as she calmly stood there. They didn't speak, and it seemed she was happy with the plant's progress.

After what felt like forever, the plant made a sucking noise and released her arms, making a weird jiggly movement, and Dae nearly threw up again. Ashlyn turned to the sink to wash her arms, which were covered in blood but not bruised or broken in any way. He scoffed the beer and tried to act like nothing had happened. By the time dinner was served, he had a million new questions, most about the killer plant.

He didn't think he would be that hungry, though, and it wasn't just the sight of his mother covered in blood that was killing his appetite. It was more about his sister. He hadn't spoken to her in ages, and now she was leaving any minute for her trip. He decided at the last second to call her and wish her well. Absently, he plucked his phone out of his pocket, just as it started to ring loudly.

Fumbling with it, he answered and said loudly, "Hang on a sec, dropped the bloody phone," before he managed to get it to his ear.

"Oh, Dae, you're a goose!" Kitty giggled, and he smiled automatically.

"What the hell, Kitty? Mom says you're going away. Without telling me? What's that all about?" He put as much gruffness into his voice as he could, so she knew he was in his annoyed big brother mood.

She sighed. "Yeah, that's why I called. I didn't want to leave without you knowing. It's all been kinda sudden, though. Listen, Dae, we touched on this a while ago, before Jess. Anyway, I owe you an explanation. We have allies, strong ones, lots and lots of them, and I know where they are, but I can't tell the others yet. It must be kept secret. I'm telling you because you aren't there and won't be for a while so there won't be any questions or anything. I've put together a team. They're the ones who are gonna help us win this war, Dae." She sounded so sure of it. What did she know that he didn't? "I'm taking them through the netherworlds to our safe zone, where they'll start training with Dale and the Great Ones, along with some other allies we've been working with."

"You...you know them? And where they are? Why haven't you said anything to the others? What the hell!" How...when had she met the Great Ones and this Dale?

Escape

"Look, it's kind of complicated, but they saved me from the Qualterra and trained me. *Before* I fell into a rip and landed here, Dae."

He had been right; there was a lot she hadn't said about what she'd gone through.

"We need to talk about this when you get home, Kitty. I need to know what happened to you. All of it, not just the edited version. I have the right to know."

"Promise. We will talk, and I will tell you all of it. Okay?" She hung up.

Dae sighed. This was all getting really complicated, really fast. He wanted to slow down, go back to being clueless and happily caring for his family. But in all honesty, he hadn't been *happily* doing that. He'd been watching his sister wither and die a slow, horrific death, and there'd been nothing he could do to make it any better for her. It had been torture, for him and Ashlyn.

Chapter 12

Q UALTERA

Lilah led the way into the Qualterra. She'd already cleared her path with Travis and the other leaders, telling them she was taking the team to the megalithic site so she could better inspect the columns and the pictures carved into them. The others had said they couldn't offer protection, so her new teammates had stepped in to 'offer' their help. It had all been a ruse to get everyone she needed there with her. Since she had a full escort, there was no need for other A.S.U members to be sent, which meant they wouldn't have to worry about anyone else checking on them.

They were going to Halla—which she hadn't told the others because she worried that some might slip up. She was excited to see her friends again, especially Dale. She worried he wouldn't remember her, but her excitement was stronger than the anxiety. She found the stairs quickly and rushed up them. Her legs burned long before she reached the top and several of her team complained about how fast she was going. She leaned forwards, resting her hands on her knees while she drew in ragged breaths. By the time she'd caught her breath, the others were just getting to the temple floor. She sat, patiently waiting for them to gather themselves.

Escape

"Okay, so, we're going in there." She pointed at the overlarge double doors at the other end of the temple. "There are lots more stairs, though. Sorry, guys." Moans filled her ears.

"Aww, shit. Come on, Lilah, we don't wanna do more stairs," Caleb whined.

"Shut it, dumbass." Emma punched him on the arm.

"Oww." Caleb rubbed his arm and moved away from Emma.

"Guys, training is gonna be much harder than this, trust me. And the best part, Mirren, your dad will be there." She grinned hugely at the dragon sulking by the foot of the staircase, and he blinked rapidly in shock.

Lilah didn't want any more distractions so she headed to the doors and set about opening them. The others followed her, speechless. She smiled a little to herself at the thought of their shock at learning a Great One would be there, that they would get to meet one of them. She didn't dare tell them how many Great Ones there were in Halla; they would probably burst into flames or something.

The large doors creaked and groaned then slowly swung open. Sulfureous air rushed out with such force that they were all taken aback by it. The res lit, just as they had when she had first come to this place. She sighed, and the sound reverberated around the chamber amidst the others' stunned silence.

Not bothering to look back at her companions, she started down the stairs. They were as wide as she remembered, though she'd somehow thought they would seem smaller now. They quietly made their way down, hugging the inner wall while flames burst into life along the outer wall and travelled downwards ahead of them. As they entered the cavern, Lilah paused. Should she announce their arrival?

A moment later, she realised there was no need. The growling and howling of wind started below, growing in volume as the seconds ticked by. They were all standing out on the narrow path now, and everyone except Lilah huddled together.

The loud *woosh* roared, and several large dragons unfurled themselves in the nooks all around the cavern. Lilah breathed a sigh of relief. Finally, she felt like she'd come home. The deepest growl started in front of them all, and Lilah smiled as she turned to the ancient white dragon with golden eyes. *Mierden*. It took all her willpower not to rush forwards, to embrace the giant. Would he even know her after all this time? Besides, Mirren would want to greet him as well.

"Hello, Mierden. I've missed you greatly, my mentor."

He paused, looking at her strangely. "Youngling?" he asked. "Is that you? You vanished many years ago. We searched all of the Qualterra for you. Dale still looks, even now. Who have you—" He stared wide-eyed at his son, still in human form, then half-stood to get a closer look. "*Mirren*? My son. I am so relieved. I feared we would never again meet. Come, all of you. We will leave for Halla immediately. Dale is hosting a large community feast tonight, a remembrance for all those lost over these years." He walked slowly, leading the way.

The other dragons murmured in their native language, the guttural sounds Lilah remembered so clearly now. As they walked along the narrow passages, Mierden offered small titbits of information about their destination. Emma and Hannah asked a few questions, and they were answered gently, as though Mierden were trying not to frighten them. The others simply

117

Escape

listened and gave short answers when asked questions but didn't elaborate or try to maintain the conversation. She knew that dragons in their natural form were very intimidating, but she'd somehow forgotten to be intimidated. Perhaps because she'd spent so much time here and had learned to know them as a people.

After a long walk, the passageway widened, with light coming through from the edges, as though they were in a tunnel with skylights. Finally, they rounded another bend and it opened into a large eld, with mountains and a river in the background. Homes dotted the landscape, blended with the surrounds so seamlessly they almost looked naturally formed. The sounds of sword- fighting reached them as they stepped out into the eld, and then there were giggles and chatter from the opposite direction.

Mierden led them to the village closest to the netherworld—the village she'd lived in with Dale and a few other families. The modest cottages seemed to grow as they wound their way deeper into the village. Vines, grass, and flowers covered them, and trees lined the cobbled streets. This was the world hidden by Aggaron, to save the last of an ancient race, now a home to all who needed one.

Lilah relaxed more, listening to the chatter of her team, and the dragons as well. A soft burbling sound came from the river as it trickled gently over rocks and water grass swished happily. She reached the cottage that was her and Dale's. The small fence was overgrown with Starling Trumpets in three different colours, and the vines that wound over the face of the cottage were covered in tiny, pink flowers that smelled like marshmallows and cookie dough. They were edible but tasted more like a bitter herb. Dale often used them to flavour stews and other spicey dishes. The windows were ajar, and what had been her room was now filled with charms. Dale was a very superstitious man, and each of those charms were a prayer for her safety. Such an incredible soul. She sighed then jumped when Hannah spoke; she hadn't realised anyone was paying attention to her.

"Are you all right, Lilah? You seem kind of...sad." She glanced from Lilah to the cottage then back again.

"I'm okay. Listen, we need to rest and eat before we start training. I'm gonna stay here. We should all find quarters. We can meet at the feast later." She turned to the others as she said it, and they all nodded.

The dragons would be the perfect distraction for them, so she didn't feel any guilt about needing some alone time. As they walked off, Lilah moved forwards, an automatic reaction to coming home, and she pushed the decorative front door open gently. It was exactly as she remembered it: the small hallway with side tables and a wall-mounted rack for coats that was more often used to hold swords and other weapons. The rugs were handwoven by locals and hinted at colours of pale blues, greens, and pinks.

Off to the right was her bedroom. She stopped in the doorway; hundreds of prayer charms hung from every wall. Her oversized bed was the same as it had been the day she vanished, not even made up. Her handmade teddy was still on the floor where she'd dropped it in her rush to have breakfast. She walked in and picked it up, hugging it tight. Then she continued down the hall. Dale's bedroom was on the opposite side of the hall and then the living room was at the very end. Beyond that was another hall that led to the bathroom and kitchen. Another small building out the back held two extra rooms, a laundry, which was

Escape

also the storeroom, and Dale's workshop where he made his weapons.

She made her way into the kitchen and put the kettle on to heat. She would make tea; it was almost time for Dale to come home, after all. He never strayed from his routines. He said they were essential and helped him feel at ease. Well, today his routines were going to be shot to hell. Lilah only hoped he would know her. She found tea in a large decorative jar on the high shelf near the window, and the teapot she'd made for him as a gift was set on the bench already. She was touched; he was using her gift. She placed twigs of tea into the tea holder and added some calming flowers then set it on the counter.

When the water boiled, she poured it into the teapot then dropped the holder into the water to steep. She was looking for teacups when she heard the door. She stood dead still, her heart pounding, and she was nearly crying she was so emotional. Footsteps made their way up the hall, and the front door snapped shut then opened again a minute later. She stared at the hall; he would be walking in any second now. Lilah couldn't have moved even if she'd wanted to until she saw his shadow and nearly broke into a sprint. *No.* It had been an awfully long time and he might panic before realising it was her. She locked all her muscles in place and stared as he came into view, his head down.

* * *

Dale glanced up as he entered his kitchen then backtracked. He wasn't alone. This was a safe place, he knew that, but it was still a shock that someone was in his home. He paused then looked at the woman closely. He blinked a few times, trying to figure out if he was crazy now.

"Papa," she whispered, and he knew her. *He knew her.* His daughter, she was here.

"How? Where were you...? We searched everywhere... Are you alright? Oh, my little one." He was struggling to get the words out, and he rubbed his hand through his hair, frustrated that he couldn't speak properly.

Tears welled in his eyes as he realised, she was crying, and he rushed forwards to hug her. His child. She held him tight and buried her face in his shoulder, her tears falling onto his shirt. He laid his open hand on her back to soothe her and nuzzled her hair. She smelled of berries.

"You made tea." He chuckled after another minute, and she giggled into his neck.

"Yes, I did. It's probably awful, though." She pulled back and wiped her eyes with the back of her hands, just like when she was a little child.

He smiled at her gently then went to get some biscuits he'd made earlier that morning. He set them on the table along with honey then waited for her to join him.

* * *

She sat, tucking her leg under her, and poured the tea. There was so much to talk about, but she didn't know where to start. He seemed to sense her tumultuous thoughts and nodded in understanding.

"We have plenty of time to talk about what happened when you're ready, little one. For now, let's celebrate your return, and later, we'll feast." He raised an eyebrow at her, and she nodded. Of course he knew her feelings. He always had. He had raised her after all.

Escape

"I found my other dad recently," she blurted.

"That's wonderful. Is he well?"

"I guess. He's different to you, though." She shrugged.

It bothered her that she hadn't told Matt about Dale, and at first it was because she hadn't remembered. But then, she'd started to bond with him and didn't know how to tell him that she remembered that but not tell him everything else, and she didn't know if he would be okay with her having another dad too. He'd struggled with hearing about her adoptive mother, though he'd tried to hide his discomfort. She didn't feel the need to hide it from Dale, though. He wasn't the kind to be upset by the news. She peeked at him and wasn't surprised to see him smiling broadly.

Chapter 13

As the sun was setting, a buzz of activity started. At first it was a gentle hum then it grew until everyone felt it. Caleb, Soren, Rylen, and Mirren were staying closest to the village square, though bunking with three dragons was slightly alarming for Caleb. He'd agreed to it because there was also a tavern next door, and after all the things that had happened lately, he wanted a few drinks.

The girls were staying on the outer edges of the village, closer to the caves the Great Ones preferred. They disliked their human forms but would take them for tonight's feast. Though it seemed everyone was attending, nobody had seen Lilah since they'd arrived, and nobody dared ask. She had assured them all they would meet up, and as she was their boss now, kind of, they trusted her word. People were piling into the large square, tables and chairs were placed all over with longer tables set around the edges. Everyone had dishes with them and set them along the tables that boarded the dining area. As the only ones who didn't bring food, the team felt a little awkward, but quickly recovered as they were welcomed with open kindness.

It was impossible to know how many different species of beings were here, but it didn't matter anyway. The adults chatted happily, and children ran between them, playing and laughing. Some people were curious and asked endless questions, and others simply stared at them. There was no malice in the stares, though, so it didn't feel weird.

Escape

* * *

Lilah and Dale walked slowly to the square, chatting about the happenings in Halla since she'd gone. There hadn't been as many changes as she had feared, and Dale was excited to learn he had new students to train, but after a minute, he slowed and turned to her.

"Little one, I know you want to help, but do you need to fight?" He ushed and looked sheepish.

"Of course I need to. I remembered my whole life, Papa. And the reason the Huntowra tried to kill me is the reason I *have* to fight this war. Can you trust me?" She looped her arm through his, keeping her gaze directly ahead of them. She saw the blurred outlines of lanterns and colours in the growing darkness, but she really wanted to see her team.

"I trust you. Always have. But as a parent, I will always default to protecting you. I know realistically that fighting is inevitable, and I'll absolutely train you. I'm just worried. I already lost you once, and you're the only family I have. That I know of, anyway." His shoulders slumped, and he frowned.

She patted his arm reassuringly. There wasn't anything she could say to make him feel better. He'd always struggled with not remembering who he was before he'd been brought here, along with the unanswered questions that came with it. Like, why him? And who had saved him? He'd just showed up with the Great Ones, and they'd refused to say who had saved Dale. What they did say was that he was the man who could train them all. It was his destiny. The side effect of saving him was the amnesia. Nobody knew if, or when, Dale would remember anything. She wished her ability could find his family for him.

Perhaps one day. For now, he was safe and here, and that was enough.

The smells of all the different foods wafted in the air, and Lilah's belly grumbled. She was hungrier than she'd been in ages. Dale had a basket loaded with vegetable bakes and a stew she'd loved. It was made from an animal very closely related to cows called an elack. The meat was darker and tasted like a mix between deer and cow, with a sweet, nutty aftertaste. They were popular with farmers on most worlds, and Dale had a whole herd in Halla. He was a natural at farming, as well as pretty much everything else he did. Lilah's mouth watered as they set the basket of goodies out, but before she could say anything she was called. She spun round, and Emma waved, nervously eyeing Dale.

"Oh, hey, there you are, Em. I was about to come look for you all." Lilah bounded over to her cousin.

"Ah. Yeah, here I am. Ha-ha. I was getting worried again, you know."

"Oh gosh, Emma, I'm so sorry. I never wanted to worry you. This is a safe world. I had to see…well, my papa." She gestured to Dale, who was watching cautiously.

Emma looked at him sharply then her face softened, and she smiled, tears welling in her eyes. "You have a papa?" She seemed relieved.

"Yeah." Lilah relaxed. "Wanna meet him?"

"Umm. Sure, I'd love to."

Lilah steered her cousin to Dale and paused about a foot from him. "Papa, this is Emma. My cousin. And Em, this is Dale, my papa." She watched as they shook hands then burst out

Escape

laughing when Emma grabbed his arm and yanked him into a bear hug. It was a gruff but somehow sweet gesture, and after a moment Dale returned the hug, chuckling loudly.

"Thanks for caring for her."

"Of course. She's my daughter. What else could I do?"

"I just mean I'm really happy she had someone to look after her, to love her, and be there as her family when we couldn't." She was crying now, and Dale nodded in understanding. "Whoa, okay, that was a whole lot more emotional than I planned for." She wiped her eyes. "Lilah, the others are looking for you too. Maybe we can all sit together?"

Lilah and Dale followed her to where the others were sitting.

"Damn, girl, thought you'd gotten lost." Caleb was chewing on a chunk of bread.

"Moron." Soren rolled his eyes, and Caleb started throwing pieces of the bread at him.

Hannah and Rylan were having a debate over ethics, and Mirren was looking for his father. Dale had been introduced to everyone straight away, and now he sat there watching all the newcomers with interest. Was it curiosity that made him stare or did he feel uncomfortable?

Tables were going up to get food from the buffets, and Caleb practically ran when it was his turn.

Soren snorted as they watched him disappear into the distance.

Lilah and Dale didn't hurry; the dishes would replenish themselves as needed. At the long line of tables, Lilah spooned out helpings of food, curries, and grain, coarse breads and fresh vegetables, and finally, a bowl of elack stew. She hadn't had this in so long and she couldn't help but scoff it down. Everyone loved the stew, and Caleb and Mirren decided to have a competition to see who could eat more. Dale laughed openly.

* * *

Dale was awake at dawn, enjoying the peace before everyone woke. He hadn't been this happy in, well, he couldn't really remember how long. He hummed as he made his morning meal and hot tea. How long could this peace and happiness last? He suspected not very.

His little one, who he'd affectionately named Starlight, had always had dreams of war; it often woke her and kept her from wanting to sleep again. He had decided to train her because she became obsessed with her dreams, and it was during a training session that she'd vanished. His eyes filled with tears as emotions slammed into his ribs so hard he struggled to breathe. He had let her train with a younger group that day, though she should've been with him picking berries and planting new vegetables. His hand shook as he reached for his cup, and he sucked in a deep and ragged breath, trying to force his body to calm. A creaking in the hall told him she was awake, and he got up to fill his kettle. He focused on making eggs and tea so that Starlight didn't see his tears, again.

"Morning, Papa," she mumbled as she stumbled into the kitchen, plonking down on the nearest chair.

"You slept in, little one. I wondered if I should just let you rest for the day."

* * *

Escape

"No. I need more sleep than before because my magix was being drained. It nearly killed me." She bit her lip nervously, not wanting to admit it but knowing it was important for Dale to know.

He spun round with the frying pan in hand, a look of absolute horror on his face.

She looked at him briefly then reached out and took the pan. "Ooh, I love eggs. Want some?" She smiled at her father as he sat then dished them some of the bright yellow eggs, heaping her own plate with more than she needed.

He saw her plate, rolled his eyes, and chuckled. "Well, we'd better get this done then. It's nearly time for training to start. I'll ask about it later, okay?" he added softly, and she knew he was talking about her magix draining away.

She didn't want her biological father to sound like an awful person, but he'd created the bands that had nearly killed her. No one could've known what could happen with the power bands, so she thought Dale would understand, but he could be protective. All the same, Lilah didn't want to hide anything from her papa. They ate quickly, almost a race to see who could finish first.

With full tummies, they made their way to the training grounds on the western plains. The fields here were smothered with flowers of all kinds, in every colour imaginable. It was truly a beautiful sight, and as a child it had saddened her to have so much horror in such a gorgeous and peaceful place. She sucked in the sweet smell of flowers and closed her eyes for a second, enjoying the moment.

A chinking sound reached her, and she sighed and opened her eyes again. Over in the far corner, a group had gathered already and were practicing some basic sword wielding techniques. Some of the villagers were demonstrating how different attacks could be blocked with some simple poses. It was like a dance, watching them pair up and try out the different stances. She wanted to join in, but her training was much more advanced. She would train with Dale one on one, and then they would both instruct the newcomers in preparation for the war. She felt an anxiety about what was coming. It was happening much sooner than anyone realised, and one wrong step now could cost them all their lives.

She didn't hate having the seer's gift, but sometimes she felt she couldn't really live because she was so busy seeing the future, or the major parts of it, anyway. Her magix was different from others because she had many unique gifts that didn't mix into one being. Seers, Dragons, Warriors… she had aspects of them all and more. She'd known as a child that the Huntowra were coming for her but hadn't known it would cost her so much. She'd known she would live, meet the Great Ones, and make new allies. But she hadn't known about Dale, and that had always troubled her.

He'd changed her so much and been so important to her successes that she couldn't fathom why he'd been invisible. Was she missing something about him? She'd thought that amnesia could be the reason, but now she knew that wasn't true. Others with amnesia showed up ne. Why was her father different? It was almost like there was a shield around him. It didn't make any sense. But she would figure it out eventually.

She shifted her attention back to the eld and people in front of her. It still took her a moment to realise Dale had walked off ahead; she had to run in order to catch up with him. He was smiling without looking at her, and she knew he'd been waiting

Escape

for her. They crossed the eld and headed into the thick jungle with streams and waterfalls lacing their way through the dense foliage. There was a custom-built arena here that used nature instead of stone, simulating a real-life battle eld.

Dale would head for higher ground—his instinct was to recon then act accordingly. Her own preference was to avoid the thickest violence and work her way inwards from the outer parts of battle. She'd learned in Qualterra that it was best to avoid the crushing hoard of Shrogan, but she'd been surprised on her last trip there. A few of the Shrogan had been spooked by some other predator and spun back to her. Lilah hadn't expected it and got cornered on a ledge that dropped into the underground cave networks. She'd had a choice: fight or be ripped apart. She chose the first. It was during that battle that she'd been flung to Earth. She remembered falling, and then more falling. And when she'd thought she couldn't fall further, she'd expected pain only to find a different falling. Lights, noise, electricity…then agony and blackness. She looked at Dale. He was watching her intently, and she nodded to indicate she was ready to begin. They turned in opposite directions and headed off into the jungle.

Later that evening, after a whole day of tracking and sword battles, Dale and Lilah stomped into the village to find the others. They were both curious about how training had gone for them, and they didn't want to cook a meal, so they decided to get some food from the street markets that were always open here. Smells of curry and roasting meats reached them, and they both inhaled deeply, their bellies growling in unison. They made their way to the vendors and piled different dishes into their arms then headed to the nearest bench to eat.

As they entered the park, they spotted Lilah's team sprawled out on a rug with various foods and medical supplies.

Caleb held a cold compress to his head and winced as he moved. Emma was patching a few scrapes on her arms and had her right wrist strapped. She looked fierce, and Lilah knew that pain would not stop or slow her down. Mirren was looking bored, and smug. He wasn't hurt at all and was happy about it, though they all knew it was because dragons healed much faster than other beings.

Hannah was fixing her hair but had bruises and a few cuts, which she seemed to enjoy showing off. She'd been with the local healers. Her magix would be slowly released, and she was spending this time learning how to control it without actually using it yet. In a short time, she would begin training with Lilah. She had told Amara her path in this war would be easier if she were using her magix.

Lilah looked proudly at her friends; they'd clearly given all they could today, and as training went on, they would be able to incorporate their own weapons and strengths as well. They would be able to train the villagers to use guns and the other weapons Earth was known for. They would share their knowledge of explosives and give demonstrations so everyone would know what to expect when the time came for them to be used.

She'd selected these people for a reason, and it wasn't just because she wanted to oversee their training first-hand. They were highly skilled in their chosen areas, all essential for combat. They were unaware of how important they were, or how important this was. These people would later form a new taskforce; they would help rebuild worlds that had been lost and strengthen ones that were vulnerable. For now, though, they were just hanging out. Laughing. They knew this war would be bad, but she didn't think they fully grasped how bloody and

Escape

terrifying it would get. They would witness things they would never have been able to imagine.

So...she let them have this. They needed it.

Chapter 14

UNNAMED WORLD, NEUTRAL GROUND

Peter was bored; there was no other word to describe the tediousness of this diplomatic mission. He was expected to play the part of future royal, as he had been since he was a pup. Even in his younger years, he'd understood these meetings were something he needed to be a part of. As a result, he'd made connections with ambassadors and new heads of government from all over the universe. He had reached out to them recently, knowing they needed every being to fight in this war. There were not just former allies here, they had all reached out to other worlds they knew of, bringing everyone they knew would want to help in some way. Lilah had told him this event was essential and had said she was off to gather more allies.

He trusted her, even after being separated so long. She was doing what she was meant to and getting everyone else where they needed to be for the coming battles. Being away from her made him anxious, though. He'd never wanted to be apart from her again and had told her that. She'd sighed, kissed his forehead, and promised that when it was all done, there would be no separating them again. It had felt like a goodbye, and instinct told him there was a large battle coming…soon.

So, he sat there, in a room of elders and soldiers and chiefs as they argued about how and where to lay traps for the

Escape

Huntowra. Some wanted abandoned worlds and others said that was useless because they would know it was a trap. Matthew and Peter had told them about the queen who seemed more intelligent than the rest, who had a purpose. Why else would she have embedded herself in their midst, gathering intel and causing mayhem wherever she could? These were not the actions of a mindless beast, as most wanted to believe the Huntowra were. Yet the others were sceptical, not wanting to believe or perhaps incapable of it after seeing them one way for so long. Either way, Peter wanted to be done with the meeting, and got up from the table, rolling his shoulders with frustration. The room fell silent then, and all eyes found him.

He took a steadying breath. "I need a break. Seems to me like you all think this isn't as serious as it actually is. Underestimating the enemy has been our biggest disadvantage all these years. We cannot and will not be victorious when we are ignorant and arrogant. They're not mindless. They plan attacks with accuracy, and they've been successful against some of our strongest allies. Does anyone remember the fall of the Aggaron?" He glared pointedly at each person and watched them as they registered what he was saying.

Faces fell and eyes filled with tears for the loss of their strongest ally—a huge blow in recent history. It had always been clear that the destruction of Helios had been planned, but nobody knew who'd been the mastermind. Now it was clear that the Huntowra had used their apparent dumbness as a ploy. No one had been prepared for that. Or the brutality of the Aggaron's deaths.

Looking back at it now, it was strange the Huntowra had only killed Aggaron, leaving other species of beings alone, even if they'd tried to help the victims. Evaliah had been one such being—she'd interfered, trying to save her friend, but the Huntowra had said he wasn't there for her...yet. Nobody had put the pieces together, until now. It seemed so obvious. The queen who'd posed as Angel had been setting them all up, but he couldn't figure out why. Was she the real boss in charge of them all, the one feared by their other captive? The Huntowra had had no real reason to attack—that they knew of, anyway. If they could figure out what was really driving their agenda, they might have a chance of stopping them.

There was chatter around him as the delegates finally started to see the real danger. Talks shifted to how they could better support each other instead of calling each other silly names for sharing ideas. This was why he was here. People listened to him without really meaning to. Matt glanced at him and lifted the corner of his mouth. He thinned his lips silently in response then ignored the older man, choosing to focus on the tactical ideas being put forward.

"Well, my people aren't the best fighters, but we sure can hide. Is there a way we can provide safe havens and act as scouts for other teams? We really want to help in a way that's beneficial to all," one man said quietly, and Peter smiled at him warmly.

"That's great. We'll need scouts and safe spaces to heal the injured and regroup. Having all kinds of skills will be essential. Don't feel embarrassed that you aren't warriors like other beings. You will provide in ways they cannot."

The man's head and shoulders lifted, clearly feeling better knowing he was able to offer meaningful help.

"My people are good with food and medicines. We've already begun making supplies for medical facilities and

Escape

medications. Some of us are warriors, and those will fight with everything we have." It was a declaration spoken confidently.

"We be fighters, and we fight. Count us all in," a brusque, wiry-haired man announced.

Affirmations came from all groups; even Earth announced their support. There was murmuring and curiosity after their declaration. Most other species didn't know them at all. But they did appreciate the support, and the chance to make some new friends.

By the end of the day, the atmosphere was completely different, and they all left feeling energised. Peter was even laughing as he sat for dinner, and he ate with gusto. Matt always ate heartily, and tonight was no different. If you didn't know who he was, you wouldn't know he was a royal at all. He was humble, got his hands dirty, and didn't complain. He always insisted that others were cared for before him, and he wasn't happy unless he was tinkering with his latest invention. They ate silently then said their goodnights. The next two days would be as challenging as today but for different reasons. Tomorrow, they would choose the main world for battle, and from there they would plan logistics.

The morning came too fast for Peter; he wanted to stay asleep a little longer. It had been a long time since he'd slept deeply, so he wanted to lap it up while he could. He dressed casually and ate some toast, not even tasting it. He wished now he'd brought coffee with him. It was sad and amazing how much he enjoyed the beverage; it reminded him of an herbal root grown on Haven. He sighed and rolled his shoulders to release the tension before today.

He'd thought long and hard about what world would be the best to stage their main assault from, and only one made sense to him. It was unacceptable to sacrifice a species and their world, but one species, one world was indestructible: the Shrogan. They needed more than one world as a base, though, as they would have to attack simultaneously from several places in order to thin out the Huntowra and reduce their advantages. The worlds had to be well-protected, abandoned, and have the ability to use magix. Helios, Qualterra, and a few other worlds would be best.

He strode out of his room and headed downstairs to the lobby, where he'd arranged to meet up with Matt—who was already there and waiting for him with an expression of anticipation. The entire atmosphere today was different, with everyone chatting excitedly. As Matthew and Peter entered, all talk stopped and everyone took their seats and waited expectantly. This was his cue. Matthew's relaxed attitude meant that although the others respected him and his position, they didn't look to him in this time as the voice for all beings. It was Peter's authority they responded to, though he wasn't sure why.

"Today, we're going to plan out where we'll host our base stations. We need more than one, and we need places that aren't endangering lives, so worlds that are abandoned but not otherwise deserted. They need to believe we're trying to reinhabit these worlds. But for the main one…I've thought long and hard about this, and I believe it should be the Qualterra."

Several delegates whispered and cast wary looks, and Peter knew why.

"Look, the Shrogan are immortal. They don't like us, but they always attack the Huntowra if we're all present in their world. I think their magix is more noticeable than ours or feels

Escape

different to them in some way. When it comes down to it, the Shrogan are going to do what they do best. They love battle, the world has no innocent beings unable to protect themselves, and we will have another advantage: the ravines will limit their ability to y and attack. Does anyone have any questions yet?"

"What happens if the Shrogan attack us instead? We can't know for sure that they'll target our enemy. It's a huge risk. Makes me nervous...but I see why you thought of it. It's bloody genius."

"He's right. It's genius. We've been monitoring the Shrogan for some time now. They use gestures and grunts to communicate, and we've started to recognise some of the meanings. We could maybe try to communicate to them that an attack is coming."

"What kind of gestures? On Earth, sign language is fairly common. Maybe I can have a look. I happen to know a few people who use sign language."

The chatter started up again.

"All right everyone, these are all great ideas. So, Terk and Jacob will try to organise a way to communicate with the Shrogan, but either way, this is the plan. Now, other bases. I know of one, but we need two or three more." He took a deep breath, knowing what reaction he would get from this suggestion. "I really feel like the backup base, the one we use to coordinate from...should be Helios."

The air changed in an instant, and you could've heard a pin drop, it was so silent. Faces fell. Nobody knew what to say.

"The Aggaron were better prepared than anyone for an attack from the Huntowra, but they were caught off-guard by them. They didn't anticipate that the Huntowra could sneak past the wards, or that they were that organised. But *we* know it's a possibility. We also know that most of the Aggaron were killed in the outer parts of Helios. The cities themselves are mostly intact...untouched by battle. There are some indications of the Huntowra in the city itself, but recognisance shows us that it wasn't their focus. That means it could make an effective base. Not only that, there are supposedly weapons on Helios that we can use against the Huntowra."

Everyone stared at him like he was crazy, but they had to know he was right. It was common knowledge that the Aggaron were advanced, had weapons no other planet had, and the best warding systems ever designed.

"Well, I like tinkering, and my wife was Aggaron. If anyone can get the wards back online, it's me." Matthew spoke softly but clearly, and Peter felt a surge of relief.

At his declaration, the others started to talk about other possible bases, and Jacob leaned into Matthew and Peter and said quietly, "Get Travis and Jeff to go to Helios with you. They both want to go there anyway after...you know, Seth," and he turned back to the rest of the delegates and joined in the conversation.

Peter and Matt exchanged a dark look but nodded. They were the best.

At lunch that day, Peter was sitting, not really thinking of anything, when he got an intense bubble of anxiety in his belly. Something wasn't right. He couldn't place it, but he felt like he was being watched. He looked around, but there was nobody watching him. He ate quickly and rushed back into the delegates' rooms. He was probably just anxious because this war

Escape

was starting to feel...*real* somehow. It was odd. He'd known his entire life that this moment would come, yet he'd had no fear or sense of urgency before. He wanted to be home, with Lilah, planning his dull transition into the world of politics and royalty. Throughout the afternoon, he tried to put it in the back of his mind, but the strange knot of anxiety wouldn't unravel.

The plans were finalised, and the delegates said their goodbyes and portaled out to inform their own peoples of the plans.

They'd already decided to use Helios and Qualterra. It also made sense to use Cree, a world that was mostly rainforest. But there was another world whose name had been forgotten; they decided to call it Serenity. This world had belonged to an ancient race of beings who'd slowly spread out then disappeared. They were called the Creators. Their magix was so ancient it had created all other magix, and historical studies had proven that these beings were real, flesh and bone and blood. For the longest time, Serenity had been destroyed, in ruins, but at around the time of Lilah's disappearance, the world had somehow revived and was flourishing. There was a wonderful energy in Serenity now —everyone who visited felt a strong sense of peace. The native wildlife was plentiful, though not yet sentient. A team of scouts had recently used the world as a shelter out of necessity...and brought it to the attention of A.S.U. They'd hoped to keep this world a secret, and a taskforce had been sent to build wards and other safety features to protect it from the Huntowra.

It was an Earth tactic to control what intel was released and to whom, and it worked very well. This was the first time this group were using it. In the group meetings, all delegates had been given the same information, but in private, each delegate had been told individual information essential to their own situation and role.

It was explained to each that they could tell nobody else in order to stop the enemy from finding out the whole plan, and they had respected it. Terk, in particular, had applauded this decision, saying that it was the trickiest but most brilliant idea ever. Terk, though, thought a lot of Earth's behaviours were that, given their evolutionary stage was similar. In fact, Terk's people were slightly more advanced technologically but lacked the ability to think outside the box, which was a common aw among magix beings. He'd formed a close bond with Jacob, and they'd both left together to get started on trying to communicate with the Shrogan.

Matt needed to return to Earth then move on to Meakra. The repairs were nearly complete, and they were using the castle as another secret base of operations. They hadn't told any of the delegates about that, figuring that keeping the numbers small would be less suspicious than marching in an army. They were planning to blindly bring heads of governments to the castle in the event of a major attack, in order to keep their respective worlds from being left without leadership. This was a backup to the backup plan though, and they'd prepared for many beings to be there at once by sending multiple teams in to check on the palace, thereby having a constant ow of magix on Meakra. The surge during the changeovers would be seen as normal by anyone looking at the levels of magix. It would be just another batch of teams replacing the last ones.

Peter and Matt were about to leave the neutral world where they'd held the meetings, but something was off.

"What?" Matt looked around them, like he'd heard something.

Escape

"You okay?" Peter asked with raised eyebrows.

"Ah...I think we're being followed."

"Shit...I thought the same earlier. I tried to push it aside, but I have this bad feeling, and it won't go away. Let's get out of here before it's a fight."

They both nodded grimly and left.

As they did, Peter looked back and swore he saw a Huntowra standing there looking at him with an expression of...well, boredom. He mentioned it to Matt as they sealed the portal, and the older man looked at him in horror; he hadn't seen it.

"We should warn all the delegates and tell them to be on guard. For now, let's focus on getting this battle underway." He sighed and looked absently ahead. "I wonder if my children have returned yet."

"No idea. Dae should be. Lilah said she was meeting up with allies and doing some special training with the team she assembled."

"*What?* What do you mean? Why wasn't I told about this?" Matt glared at Peter with such intensity that he stepped back.

"Don't be crabby at me. You and I just did the exact same thing to the delegates. She knows more than any of us, and we need to trust her instincts. Remember what happened last time someone tried to stop her using her magix as it was meant to be used?" Peter snapped back then instantly felt guilty when Matthew cringed. That wasn't fair, he knew it wasn't, but it was too late now to unsay it. Peter gulped then mumbled, "Shit, sorry. That was completely uncalled for. You wanted to protect your child and give her an actual childhood. I should never have said that, Matty."

The older man nodded. "You know what? You're right. I wanted her to be a child. I wanted her to play and giggle and be all the things little girls should be. But she was never a little girl. Not really, anyway. Even back then, you tried to tell me, and I dismissed it because I was the dad and you were a punk kid who was always there, in my way. It took me ages to see that you knew her better than anyone, so I'm gonna trust you now. It's long overdue, but still, if she said this was how things need to be then that's the plan. I'm all in." He shrugged before turning and striding off towards his office.

Peter stood there with his mouth hanging open. Did that just happen?

Travis found him still staring off into space. He had his arms full of bullet clips in crates, and he set them on the floor and groaned as he stretched his arms. "Phew, that's a relief. These suckers are heavy. Whatcha doing? Seems like I find people staring off like that a lot lately. Need a hand or you having a moment?" He grinned.

Peter chuckled and rolled his eyes. "Dork. Hey, I actually need to chat to you. Have you got a minute?"

"Sure thing, man. Gotta get these clips to the armoury, but we can chat if you don't mind walking with me?" He raised an eyebrow at Peter questioningly then bent to retrieve the heavy clips without waiting for an answer.

Peter fell into step beside him. "I need to ask you a huge favour. Well, you, Jeff, and…and Seth. We need you to come to Helios with just a few of us, a small squad. We need to find out how many weapons there we can salvage, and Matty is gonna

Escape

try get the wards up and running again. Helios is a huge powerbase for us. We need this, Travis." He looked almost pleadingly at Travis, who was suddenly pale, but after a moment, he agreed.

"I'll have a chat with them tonight. When did you wanna leave for this crazy-ass mission?"

"As soon as we can. We would be there now, if we could, but Matt needs to get some stuff settled here first, and I wanted to chat to you about it. I need you to know something else too. This plan is Lilah's. She said she saw Helios being a major strong point, and that we needed to be in control of it. We might get company while we're setting it up, so be ready for the possibility. I mean, we'd decided ages ago to try to use it as a base but then when Lilah told me about her visions, I knew it was meant to be. We want you there because you know it well. You've been to Helios so often it's basically another home for you. And I know Seth—"

"He's not gonna be forced. If he says no then we won't do it, and neither Jeff nor I will leave him."

"I know. I was gonna say we'll have him in the dense city and with you or Jeff at all times. Matt can only reach the wards from the inner city so I'll go with him as a bodyguard."

"He won't need more than you as protection?" Travis's eyebrows shot up, and he blinked.

"Trust me, I'm all the backup he'll need if it comes to it. I just prefer not to have to be…well, you know." Peter shrugged and looked away, not wanting to have this conversation.

Travis considered him for a minute then seemed to decide that Peter wasn't totally insane. "Righto. Well, I'll text ya as soon as we decide." He unlatched the armoury door and stalked inside with the crate.

Peter sighed and turned. He wanted some solitude, and the only place for that was his library.

Peter had been in his library for a few hours when his phone buzzed, and he threw papers and books everywhere trying to unbury it. Finally, after chucking a copy of dragon lore over his shoulder, he snatched up the phone and clicked the button so he could read the message.

"Hey, we talked it over. We're in. Meet us in the infirmary at 10am. Seth has a check-up before we leave. Night."

Peter sighed. It was comforting to know they would be with him tomorrow, and he responded with a single word: *"Thanks,"* before shutting his phone off and heading to his room for the night.

He stopped by the kitchens and made sandwiches, humming to himself as he did. He cleaned the benches and left with his arms full of stacked sandwiches. Did he need them all? No. Did he think he could eat them all? Also no. But he didn't know when he would be here again and able to make more, so he enjoyed a moment of gluttony. He sat in the window seat and looked out at the busy city in the distance. His room was on the top floor, so he was able to see a great deal of it. The curtains gently moved in the evening breeze, and he let them glide over his arms, feeling nostalgic about a time on Haven when he did nothing more than stare at the skies from his bedroom windows.

It was about one in the morning when he finally drifted off to sleep, and he had dreams about battles where all his loved ones were killed in front of him. When his alarm went off at

Escape

eight, he hit the snooze button and rolled over, only to be woken by a loud thumping on his door.

"*Shit*. Fuck. Hang on," he yelled as he scrambled out of bed and stumbled sleepily to the door.

He yanked it open, and almost collided with Matt, who'd decided to come in instead of waiting outside.

"Oh, hey. It's you. Sorry, I overslept. It was a shit night, and now I wish I'd gone to see a healer for a remedy. What's up?"

"Not much, really. I'm ready, and didn't know where you were so came looking... Did you manage to get Travis, Jeff, and Seth on board?"

"Ah, yeah, actually I did. Trav messaged me late last night. We gotta meet them in the infirmary in... *Fuck*, now." He glared at his clock, threw on a shirt, and grabbed his shoes on the way out the door.

He almost ran up the hallway, skidding on the smooth linoleum with his bare feet. Matthew ran behind him but only caught up to Peter at the doors to the infirmary. He rested his hands on his knees and drew in deep breaths for a moment, and Peter blushed with embarrassment. He forgot that he was a lot taller than most people, except his brothers.

"Sorry, Matt, I forgot." He shrugged, and the older man waved an absent hand at him, not worried at all.

Just then the doors opened, and he came face to face with his brother, who looked furious, but Peter had no idea why. He blinked, staring at Jeff stupidly then his mouth thinned as Travis and Seth came up behind him. Travis seemed sad, and Seth looked completely bored. Huh. Maybe Jeff and Travis were having an argument? He wanted to ask, but Jeff shook his head slightly. He was an empath, so he had a sense of what Peter was wondering, but did he mean no, they hadn't been fighting or no, don't ask yet? Deciding he should respect his brother's wishes, he shrugged and smiled at the other two, who were chatting now.

Travis grinned and picked up a full bag. "Hey, sorry we made you wait. The healers took a bit longer than we wanted."

"Pfft, yeah, that's an understatement. Took forever, bro," Seth muttered as he rolled his eyes, and Jeff glared at him for a minute before speaking.

"Remember what Eve said. If he gets any sign of sickness, we head straight back here immediately. I won't tolerate any excuses. It's non-negotiable. This is the only way I agree to going at all, and letting Seth go." Jeff was stern, looking at all of them in turn.

Oh. That was what was happening here. Jeff was protecting his surrogate. That made sense. Peter had nearly forgotten that without a spleen, Seth was much more sensitive to illness and viruses. He looked at his brother meaningfully, promising to look out for Seth too, and Jeff gave him a small smile to show he understood the message. His shoulders relaxed then, and they left for Helios.

Escape

Chapter 15

HELIOS, MAIN CITY

Helios was an absolutely stunning world. Even in disrepair, it exuded power, might, and elegance. The team portaled right into the magix ring in the centremost tower of the capital city. There weren't any actual names for the cities here, which, now that he thought about it, was kind of weird. Was it an oversight? Did the Aggaron have names for them that they simply hadn't told anyone? It was one of the mysteries of the Aggaron, but it had never bothered him before now.

Huh. Would he ever discover the answer? There were archives here detailing the history of Helios for tens of thousands of years. When all this was done, if he were still around, maybe he could dig into the historical records and see if they'd ever had names for different parts of this world.

Matt was wandering around the room, kicking debris and checking out the paper littering the room. It had been left untouched since the night of the Aggaron's destruction, and they all wondered what had happened in here in those final moments. Matt leaned down and picked up a towel, stained and scrunched up. He straightened it out, and Peter realised the staining was blood. He looked at the others with moisture in his eyes, and then Seth had an idea.

"Hey, we should check the tunnels. What if they were compromised?"

"I agree with Seth. Peter, can you come with me to check for damage and collapsed areas? Jeff and Seth can start on the armoury, and Matthew can just…chill." Travis shrugged.

"Yeah, okay. Sure. We will be gone a while, though. There are dozens of tunnels to check. Did you wanna bring an RME or something?"

"Nah, we'll come back here for dinner then head out again. It will take longer, but this way we can check in with each other as well."

"Sounds good to me. Let's do it." The two men left the room.

The halls were almost clean, no dust had settled here, and it made them anxious, as though the Aggaron would be back at any moment to imprison them for trespass. It was a surreal feeling. At the end of another long hall was a solid stone door. It was different from the cathedral-style buildings this world was full of. This architecture was older somehow, and yet it melded almost seamlessly with the newer buildings surrounding it. Peter rested a hand on the stone door, a plain-looking chunk of rock held in place by iron brackets and a matching door ring.

The door creaked and opened, a cold draft escaping into the hallway and giving Peter goosebumps because the door opening so easily meant that the wards hadn't just been damaged, they'd been switched off altogether. This was worse than damage; it meant that the enemy had intimate knowledge of how to use Helios's tech.

Escape

Would they be able to defend against the weapons as well? He needed to discuss this with the others, all together. But for now, they needed to make sure the tunnels were cleared, more so since the wards weren't on. It would be unbelievably bad for them all if there were Huntowra hiding here in the tunnels, waiting to kill them in their sleep.

They walked in silence, shining lights in all directions as they went. The interior of the tunnels was as beautiful as the exterior—large window openings were evenly spaced along the entire length. After an hour, they reached the first ward post.

"Damn, it's like a giant lighthouse but attached to a crap tonne more of them. This is some seriously cool stuff, Peter. Like a science fiction movie or something."

"Do you watch a lot of those then?"

"Nah, but enough to know this is some serious tech and not just magix. See these? They're power cables. They'll run throughout all the wards and tunnels. My guess is that the Aggaron didn't just rely on their magix to keep them safe. Look, here's a control box. If I just..." He popped open a small square box. "Yep, eureka. *Shit*. See this." He indicated with his torch, and Peter looked interestedly at it. What did he see that Peter didn't? "That's the wiring for this room. And someone's cut them. This wasn't a case of the enemy sneaking past the wards. This was deliberately cut to let the army in." He looked at Peter in horror, and Peter paled.

"We need to check the rest. If they're all the same, we need to assume the Huntowra know the tech of Helios very well, and that's not good for us. If they know this, they could know how to defend against the weapons we hope to use against them as well." He was exasperated now—just when he thought they could get the upper hand, something like this happens.

The two men moved on and checked three more towers, but only one of those had been tampered with. That was good news, and Travis said Seth knew how to x the wiring so he could show Matt how to do it. They didn't know why all the towers were down if only some had been tampered with, but Travis speculated that it might be because they relied on a percentage of them to be in working order for all of them to function.

A few relied on solar power, some on fossil fuels, and some ran on batteries. If you had a battery bank, for example, and one or two of seven batteries failed then the others still generated enough to keep the lights on. But if three or more failed…well, no power. It made sense when he thought about it, but again, his people's biggest aw was that they didn't consider these things, relying on magix.

Travis took photos of the wiring inside all the boxes so Seth could figure out how to x them then the pair made their way back. Only one tunnel had some minor damage, but that seemed to be from years of disuse rather than battles. Travis wondered out loud how Peter came to this conclusion, and Peter replied, "Well, there aren't any scorch marks or bodies." A dark and macabre statement, yet it was true; there were no actual signs of fighting in the tunnels.

They found Matt, Seth, and Jeff looking over some weapons they'd retrieved from the armoury, checking them for damage. The guns were like large rifles, but in place of bullets there was a speaker to *'take away their wings'* as Lilah had suggested months ago. She'd been thinking along the same lines as the Aggaron, it seemed. How strange that other beings hadn't

Escape

really considered something so simple to gain the upper hand against the Huntowra.

"So, we point speakers at them and then what?" Seth was confused.

"They probably rely on certain frequencies to fly, so if we disrupt that, we get them on the ground with us, which is an advantage…" Jeff started to explain.

"How's that a bloody advantage?"

"They rely on the air for attacking. Put them on the ground, and they can't manoeuvre as well as they can if they're up in the air." Matt was the one to answer. "Besides, they aren't as good at hand-to-hand combat as they are with aerial attacks."

Seth seemed to think about this for a moment then shrugged and went back to checking the weapons.

"We have good news and bad news about the wards," Travis said. "The good news is that we'll get them up faster than we thought we could. Now for the bad." Everyone looked at him, waiting expectantly. "The wiring was cut in a few of the towers we inspected so far. Someone deliberately cut the power to the wards. The Huntowra knew how to take them down, and they didn't use brute force to do it." They all looked at each other, understanding what that meant. "Either they had someone inside Helios working with them, or they know Aggaron tech a lot better than we anticipated."

Everyone was silent; even the breeze outside seemed to hush at his words.

There were fifteen towers surrounding this city—and every other city on this world, but they only needed to get the wards up in the capital for now. They'd do the rest later if they needed to. They ate quietly. All of them were tired and had a lot to worry about.

Seth and Matt were going over the wiring images, but it soon became clear that Seth wanted to do it himself.

Matt suggested that in the morning he and Peter take over searching the central tower for more useful stuff, and Jeff reluctantly agreed. He was going with Seth no matter what, so if he wanted to do the wiring job, they would do it together.

"And I can come and keep you company too," Travis announced.

Jeff ushed a little, seeming pleased.

It was an early night, with Travis and Seth needing sleep. Matt lay down to rest, but Jeff and Peter just sat there, still as statues. It was peaceful, with no noise to distract them from listening to the night. It sounded different to the day, though it couldn't be heard with human ears. A low humming sound, like a song caressing their ears, was constant, and reminded them of water owing over rocks. The air sounded electric. It was magix they heard, as they did on all worlds that had it—an excited kind of sound, but instead of cutting over the top of the night song, it seemed to work around it. It was as though the air and night were singing a duet. Peter smiled to himself, and his brother did the same.

They sat there the whole night just letting the sounds soothe them. As the sun came up, Travis snored loudly, and Jeff looked at him with surprise. Peter laughed; it was a quiet sound, but it caught his brother's attention. He glared at Peter, knowing his thoughts, and then determinedly looked anywhere else. Peter felt a surge of happiness, being able to tease his brother. It wasn't

Escape

long until the others woke, though, and then they were all busy getting ready for today's tasks.

After Seth's team headed out, Peter and Matt started to explore the central building. There were endless passageways, and larger ones spiralled off and out into the nearby buildings. Windows lined with coloured glass images made the walkways shine in different colours and glistened in the sunshine. They checked all the doors they could open. Some were used for storage, and some were just empty rooms, like conference rooms. A few were locked, and it felt like an eternity before they reached the last door. They both stopped in front of it, breathing a sigh of relief before opening it. The air here was stagnant, and the room was dark. There were no windows in this room, which was odd because every other room had floor to ceiling windows, even the storage rooms.

What was weirder, though, was that this sealed room wasn't in the basement; it was on the highest floor. The two men moved into the stagnant air; it was so thick you could feel it trying to choke you. In the centre of the room was a chair with chains stretching up and around it. A torture room, maybe? Why did the Aggaron need one at all? There wasn't much else to see in the room, and it was darker than any cell on Haven, which was infamous for its prisons. Matt tripped on a pile of rags near the far wall.

"Oh, my stars, what the hell?"

"What is it?" Peter shone his light at the other man's feet.

His blood ran cold. There was a bone in the rags. No, not a bone…a skeleton. A prisoner had been left here, and probably died of starvation locked in this darkened room.

As he moved the light upwards, it became clear that these were Huntowra remains, and it made sense then why there were no windows here. Peter didn't feel sad for it, but he did think it was strange that the Aggaron were holding one of the Huntowra here, especially given their kill-onsight stance regarding them. And stranger yet, it wasn't chained to the chair. It had been free to move about the room. Odd. Why would the Aggaron have let it loose?

"Let's report to the others. They'll want to know about this, Matt."

"Yeah, there's a few things I'd like to know about it, too," Matt said darkly, and he turned away without another glance.

"How long do you think they'll be gone for? We could go find them," he suggested.

"Sure, that's a good idea. Let's go now. This place is giving me the creeps."

Peter shivered, following Matt into the hall.

They were both quiet on the way to the others, still thinking about the windowless room. They found them at tower number seven, having restored the first ones fairly easily.

"See this? It's like someone tried to patch it here, but they were either in a hurry or didn't know what they were doing. They got it all back to front."

"Okay, whiz kid, just get to fixing it. We don't need the commentary about the failings of an extremely advanced race of beings." Travis rolled his eyes dramatically.

Peter and Matt both chuckled, and Seth looked round, grinning like a kid with his favourite toy. "Hey, guys, been there long?"

Escape

"Nah, just long enough to hear you bagging out the Aggaron," Peter quipped.

"Ah. Yeah, you heard, huh? Look, I just meant—"

"I know. It's okay, actually. Listen, guys, we need to talk a minute." Peter gestured for Matt to take charge.

"We found something. Most of the rooms are empty or filled with linens and paper and stuff that's not really important. But there's one windowless room on the very top floor, and there's a dead Huntowra in it. Looks like the thing might have starved to death, but it wasn't chained. Looks like they were gonna move it but then didn't."

"Wow, that's gross, dude."

"I'm more worried about why it's even there at all, actually. The Aggaron were strict about killing Huntowra on sight, so why would they have one locked in a tower room?"

"Well, sounds kinda brutal, but you know, how else do you safely test weapons on them for effectiveness? I mean, it makes sense they would want to try the things out. Better to do it in a controlled environment than when a Huntowra is sneaking up on you to abduct, torture and…" Seth spluttered off into incoherent muttering, leaving the others to look at each other in confusion.

Had they really used the Huntowra like that? It seemed the Aggaron hadn't needed to resort to things like that, but when he thought about it, it made sense. But then why unchain it only to leave it in the room to die? That was just so weird. He pondered this often as they continued to work on the towers, which took another two days. After finishing the last tower, they decided they would all go look at the skeleton last, to see if there was any evidence of testing on it. Before he had joined A.S.U, Travis had wanted to work in forensics. He hadn't completed his training, but he remembered a fair bit and was con dent he would be able to tell.

"All right, folks, now to find the on switch. The control room has to be linked to the towers, so we need to find somewhere that's powered but not where we've been. Any ideas? Anyone?" Travis looked at each of them and waited for someone to answer.

"Erm, what about the basements? There are two of them. One's a storeroom for furnishings and art, but the other one we couldn't get into. It's got an access door in the storage area, but it was sealed shut. Maybe if we can find a way in?" Matt shrugged like he wasn't sure, but it was clear to Peter, at least, that he knew this was the only answer.

"Matthew's right. I feel his surety and Peter's agreement. They just don't want to seem like know-it-alls," Jeff announced suddenly, and Peter could've smacked him.

This was payback for this morning; it had to be. Jeff smiled a little, his eyes sparkling, and ignored his brother. Seth snickered and grabbed his bag. Clearly, he thought Jeff was being funny. Peter wanted to understand the bond they shared. It seemed that Jeff was changing as much as Seth. Did surrogating work like that? The bond meant they were connected—emotionally, at least—but the rarity of surrogating meant there wasn't a lot known about it in general. He kept his thoughts to himself—except for Jeff, of course— and they made their way to the basement level.

The whole basement was filled with treasures, and they stayed together and moved carefully through it so they didn't

Escape

damage any of the history here. They were looking for the locked door they believed led to the control room for the wards. When they reached it, they took turns trying to pry it open. That didn't work. Magix didn't either. No matter how long they stood there arguing about it, the door remained firmly shut.

★ ★ ★

In frustration, Matt sat and let the younger ones fight it out.

He needed the break; he wasn't as young as he used to be, and honestly, he didn't want to fight about something he had no control over. He leaned his head against the wall and felt a slight breeze on his neck. It was nice; he focused on that as the voices blurred into a single buzzing. His eyes closed, and he was nearly asleep when it occurred to him that there shouldn't have been a breeze, let alone one along the wall. He slowly opened his eyes, looking for the source, and saw an air vent. There was a wrought iron grate locked in place over it, but he thought it was big enough for him to t through—he was a slightly smaller build than the others.

He skidded sideways to the grate and started to unscrew it from the wall. The others were still talking among themselves about how to get into the sealed floor and didn't notice what Matt was doing. He considered calling out to them but then decided it would be quicker to just check it out himself. He lifted the grate off and set it carefully aside then positioned himself so he went into the vent head first. His shoulders just t. He knew then he was small enough, his shoulders and hips were about the same width; he knew that because his man servant said it every time he was measured for a new suit. He grinned to himself. The thought of his man servant finding him inside a tiny tube made him want to laugh out loud.

P Ryall

The vent was about twelve feet long, and it was straight, so he was twisting the grate off the other side before he knew it. When the last screw popped out, the whole thing thudded to the floor, a deafening clang in his ears. The others must've heard that, and he paused for a moment, ready to tell them he was okay. But they were still talking loudly to each other. Unbelievable. He could've been murdered and they wouldn't have known. He pulled himself through and straightened, relieved to stretch his limbs.

He magixed a light, growing the orb to the size of a large watermelon, and set it to follow him. He squinted to see the back of the room. It wasn't another level as the others had thought; it was another room on the same level. The entrance made it seem that there were stairs heading down, but perhaps that was the whole point. The Aggaron kept their secrets well, so why not this one?

When he reached the door, he looked around the wall for a button or something to open it. The walls were bare, but several stations stood in the room, each filled with buttons and levers. He started to look for writing when he saw a lever with an image of a door under it. This one was yellow whereas all the other ones were grey or black or red. He shrugged and pulled the lever. A loud crack rent the air, and he ducked, thinking someone had shot at him. Then the door swung inwards and banged loudly as it locked into the open position.

"Well, that's one way to open a door, I guess. Good job, old man." Travis grinned hugely at the older man.

Matthew held his tongue between his teeth and brushed his hands on his thighs, trying to get the dust off. Jeff frowned, and Peter just stood silently at his side.

Escape

"Jesus, Trav, make a joke, why don't ya?" Seth snickered, and he strode to the console tables and started looking.

"I don't know what they're for. Could be a boom button or something, you know?" Matt joked to Seth.

"Well, yeah. I'd be shocked if there wasn't, actually. It makes sense to have a self-destruct. But I'm not looking for that. What I want is something with dials and knobs, which would be used to manage the ow of power going to the wards. Kind of like the ones inside the wire boxes, you know…the ones we talked about not playing with in case it changed a setting?" He looked at Matt, not being silly or condescending but rather with a look that showed he understood the concern but knew exactly what to do in here.

Matt nodded wordlessly and smiled, gesturing for Seth to do whatever he needed to.

They watched as Seth flitted between consoles, adjusting dials and moving switches.

An hour later, Seth stopped and wiped his forehead. The others were leaning against walls or sitting in the stools, careful not to touch anything on the consoles.

"Okay, people. Are we ready?" His eyes glistened, and he flipped a final switch.

A whirring started and built up then an electric shield went up around the walls, and the lights all switched on at once. There was a constant hum from the wards, and a screen flickered to life on the wall, showing all the towers coming online. One by one, they lit up blue, indicating they were active and functioning.

Seth clapped loudly, and they all cheered as they realised that not only were the wards here coming to life, but the entire planet's wards were coming online as well. This was more than they'd hoped for, and Seth in particular was excited by all the cool new stuff happening. He went to the screen and started to touch it before realising it was an interactive glass, the closest they had was touch screens back home. He was eyeing them from all different angles, commenting on various things. Matt and Jeff both helped to translate the language where needed, but it seemed that most of it was intuitive. Seth just seemed to know what was what.

"So, we gonna go explore some more or what?" he asked excitedly, and Travis groaned.

"No, you ninny, we aren't. Remember why we're here. You're looking for armoury stuff, and, let's face it, that stuff we found isn't all that a whole planet would have to fight a war. So, use this stuff," he gestured to all the gadgets and screens around them, "to find the rest of what we need, and we'll ensure the perimeters are secure. We're about to set this up as a base of operation, so get moving and do your damn job." He was curt but not unkind.

Peter respected that; he knew it was sometimes hard to be a leader when the ones you lead were people you loved deeply.

Seth looked somewhat crestfallen, but he turned back to the screens and started figuring out how to do a search for what they needed. Jeff would be with Seth to translate, and Travis would be checking the outer perimeters on his own. With the wards back online, it was much safer. Peter and Matt left them to it.

Escape

Travis went off in the opposite direction to the others and wandered casually, checking for signs of breaches and marking any potential weak spots. The outer edge of the forest was the limit of their safe area. They couldn't gain enough advantage by being closer to the city, and the ward towers meant they would be at a bigger disadvantage coming closer than the farmlands. He wasn't prepared to push the limits they'd declared by entering the outer farms. Everything they could need was within the forests and city, so he focused on that.

He was near the edge of the forest now, and he looked out over the elds. It was so beautiful here. The ward towers shone slightly in the night, with a slight blue-purple hue to them. He was just enjoying the quiet when he saw it. A light in the sky above the far tower, and two beings coming through it. They didn't land and seemed to be losing their ability to stay up in the air, then they left again. Quickly. He needed to tell the others, now, but before he'd done more than decide, Jeff appeared at his side.

He jumped back. "What the *fuck?* Jesus, you scared the hell outta me, Jeff. What's up? Hey, since you're here I need to tell you—"

"That the Huntowra tried to enter and were repelled by the wards. Yeah. I know. Are you okay?" He raised an eyebrow at Travis.

"Ah, yeah. Guess. How'd you... Never mind. Seth and the damn gadgets," he concluded, and Jeff nodded grimly. "They were always gonna know about it. I guess it's no different if it's today or in a week, right?" He was still trying to slow his heart, and he looked at Jeff solemnly.

Jeff just looked straight back to him. After a minute that seemed like forever, he held out a hand to Travis, and not really knowing why, he took it without a word. In an instant, they were both back in the central building with the others. Seth had a tablet-looking device and was monitoring things from it, Matt was stuffing his face with some kind of meat, and Peter was looking through some papers he'd found somewhere. Nobody seemed worried, so why was Jeff so serious? And where had they gotten meat from? It sure smelled great. Travis's belly growled loudly. He hadn't realised how hungry he was.

Matt laughed a little and handed him a skewer with what looked like a large turkey leg. He bit into it and his eyes watered; it was really hot. Then he tasted the flavour—it was the sweetest meat he'd ever tasted. It kind of had a honeyed ham flavour, only with the melt-in-your-mouth texture of slow-cooked pork. He ate it within seconds then burped loudly, causing everyone to laugh. It was a pleasant evening, and the only serious talk was about the Huntowra spying on them. The others felt that it was ne the Huntowra had seen them already, and the first batch of soldiers from A.S.U would arrive in the morning anyway.

Peter had contacted them and advised it was best to populate now that the wards had been repaired successfully. Apart from the surprise, it had happened so fast there was no concerns from the leaders. Seth continued to monitor the wards and system functions throughout the night, seeming completely comfortable, despite this being where his attack had taken place.

The morning came too fast for Travis; he wanted to sleep more. It had been hard to rest knowing where they were, and what happened yesterday evening had really worried him. He wasn't superstitious, by any means, but it felt like a bad omen or something. As a result, he'd tossed and turned all night long, not

Escape

really getting much sleep other than a few naps here and there. As they ate breakfast, Travis stared into his bowl of porridge and tried to will himself to be ne again. He noticed when Jeff sat next to him but didn't want to look up.

As an empath, Jeff knew what he was feeling, and that somehow made him more unsettled. Generally, he liked that Jeff knew all his thoughts and feelings. It had been scary at first, but now it was handy. They were able to work more efficiently because he didn't have to express his thoughts out loud; the two of them just knew what each was thinking. It was the ideal partnership, really. Every team aimed for it. But there were aspects to his emotions that he'd rather keep private. Luckily for him, so far, they'd been either ignored or unnoticed. He didn't know which and didn't want to know.

"The first three groups will arrive in about ten minutes. Perhaps you should be dressed and ready to greet them. You are the team leader, after all." He said it softly, but Travis still started at Jeff's words.

"Yeah, you're probably right. I don't mean to be so quiet, I just—"

"I know. It's okay. If you hadn't noticed, they're all worried too. They're just hiding it differently. Seth is a ball of anxiety. This is where his life changed, and he's really trying to get past what happened, but it's not as easy as just pretending it's all ne. Matt, his wife was murdered here. His son was, too, and then he discovered he was alive but doesn't remember him. All that after losing his daughter, the most beloved child in all our worlds. He's lost. His emotions make him feel like he's spinning round and round, with no way to stop. He wants to be sick it's so bad. And Peter? He's full of rage, and worry, and he's confused. Me, well I feel…overwhelmed. But that's not because of *my* fears or worries, no, it's all of everyone else's around me. I don't really know what my own feelings are yet. They're buried so deep under the mass of other stuff that I can't find them." He sighed, and Travis noted for the first time that there was a sadness to Jeff, a deep one he'd somehow missed before.

Instead of saying anything, he thought about what Jeff had told him.

Of course, everyone was worried. He'd been foolish not to see that. It wasn't just him, and he was their team leader.

He sucked in a deep breath and stood. "Thanks. I really needed to hear it, and you're right."

* * *

He left to use the restroom and freshen up, leaving Jeff to ponder his thoughts alone. Travis had thought he was sad. He'd felt the belief that he was deeply sad. Was it really sadness? It was a few minutes before Travis re appeared. He'd straightened his clothes and washed his face, slicked his hair back, and used deodorant.

"All right, everyone, we're having company real soon. Let's make 'em feel at home," he said in a loud voice.

He was about to continue, but a portal opened, and the new teams all came through. It was fairly busy then, getting everyone settled into the rooms they were turning into bunk rooms. They didn't want to use the outer buildings in case of a breach, so they stayed in the centre building. The noise that filled the halls now seemed overwhelming after the quiet of the last few days.

Escape

Chapter 16

MEAKRA

It took a week for the command centre on Helios to be fully functional, and Matthew had gone back to Meakra once everyone was settled. There were now close to sixty personnel from A.S.U living in the central tower, most from Earth. There was a buzz of excitement that just grated on Matthew. He felt like they were being dismissive of the inhabitants of Helios. It was important to show proper respect for the lives callously taken, for his wife and her family. He knew they meant no harm, but he couldn't shake the feelings in his belly.

He needed to sort out his own world, anyway, and it was better to be here, in his actual home, to do it. He wandered the hallways, looking out the numerous windows and sighing. Newly built wards surrounded the entire city, and others were being erected in the other cities as well. It hadn't taken long, once they knew how the wards worked. Magix owed into them and acted as a physical barrier, and Seth was working to add electrical components as well; they would work the same as the ones on Helios. They would have a physical and auditory barrier to help keep this world safe from further attacks. He wished he'd thought of this before his daughter's abduction. It was the beginning of his world crumbling and being blown apart.

He pushed the thoughts and memories away and strode to his bedroom. He'd never wanted to use it before; it was cold and impersonal in his mind, but as he no longer had access to his cottage, there was no other place to be. The dressing room alone was as large as his cottage had been, and the bathroom almost the same size. It was insane; the opulence and grandiosity of the castle had always made him uncomfortable.

He resigned himself to ignoring it all as he undressed and ran a hot bath. He desperately needed one. He smelled, badly. A chuckle slipped out in the quiet room as he thought of how his staff would've reacted to his odour. There hadn't been proper shower facilities on Helios, though wash sinks had made it bearable. The bathrooms here were so magnificent and well cared for, even after years of neglect. Then he felt bad for thinking less of the Aggaron. In all honesty, the tower hadn't needed shower rooms. That was their place of business, after all. All the beings that lived there had homes or farms in the outer reaches of the cities. Homelessness hadn't been a problem, either. They'd found ways to ensure that all the inhabitants had a home of their own.

Matthew sank into the bath gratefully and shut his eyes, letting the water soothe his muscles. He was happy knowing that soon the castle, *his* castle, would be filled with his people once again. And additionally, he would welcome new people into his home, friends he'd found in the harshest of circumstances. They would hold a welcome home ceremony, and then it would be straight to work.

There were lots of jobs that needed to be done. They had to organise scouts to monitor the Huntowra. Tracker teams had been arranged already, but they had to be strategically placed so they were safe yet easily accessed if needed. Healers would join

Escape

every group in the eld, and medic centres would be set up on all the worlds they were based on as well. This wouldn't be a time to celebrate in earnest; it would be the start of an all-out attack on their enemy.

He closed his eyes and tried to empty his mind of thoughts. After a few minutes of complete silence, there was a loud crashing sound, followed by voices. One was shouting, the other muted and seemingly embarrassed. He dressed using magix as he made his way out to see what had happened.

"For Christ's sakes, Flanagan, that's expensive. How you gonna pay to x that, huh?"

"How you know it's expensive? Could be that it broke before we got here anyway. Can't prove nuffin, I say."

"You're such a dolt, hey. Course they can prove it. Dumbass."

Matthew laughed, and both men jumped.

"Yep, it was expensive, but thanks to where we are, it's also… fixed." He waved his hand as he said the last word, and the vase repaired itself seamlessly and reset itself on the pedestal.

The men looked shocked. It hadn't occurred to them that it was something that could be fixed, and he wondered brie y if they were new to the A.S.U. and defence program. Then the men gaped and whooped. *Yep.* Brand new to it all. He smiled encouragingly at them then walked off as they continued to converse about the cool magic trick. He didn't feel up to educating them about the differences between magic, and magix. It wasn't important to know that, not right now.

As he walked down to the kitchens, he could hear the echoes of the men and smiled to himself. It was nice to hear sounds of happiness, even if it was only temporary. He looked about, wanting to make something then realised there was no food yet. They hadn't bothered to stock the cupboards as everyone had ready meals available. He could use magix but getting it the way humans did helped soothe his strange feeling of foreboding. It had started around a month ago and hadn't eased.

Tomorrow, he would gather as much as he could from the village gardens and orchards. The magix here meant that everything kept growing as it would with caretakers helping, and that meant there was more than enough to feed everyone. He had no doubt the others would send hunting parties out for fresh meat, and his people would teach them what was edible and what wasn't.

The next morning after he breakfasted, Matthew dressed casually. He found the boots he used for gardening and pulled them on then dug into the cupboard to find baskets for gathering flowers and other items from the markets. He was at the door to the castle grounds when the men from last night caught up with him, and he sighed in frustration.

"I'm going to gather some fresh produce from the village. It's just as safe there as it is here. I'll be back soon enough and then we can eat some real food for a change." He didn't even let them talk. He just blurted it out then strode off into the castle grounds.

Starling Trumpets grew everywhere like roses. The smell was strong and sweet, and he instantly calmed as he wandered down the paths leading to the village. There were vegetable gardens and orchards in the castle grounds as well, of course, but

Escape

he wanted to see his home again, and he wanted to be away from the suffocating splendour of the home he'd been raised in. It may look ultra-comfortable and lovely to outsiders, but to him, he felt like he'd been in a fancy prison. Nothing more.

He waved his arm absently as he reached the stone wall that separated the castle and village, and the gate opened with a soft creaking. He stepped into the village for the first time since the evacuation and stood for a minute, just taking it all in. The buildings were all the same, seemingly untouched except for the overgrowth of plant life and a thick layer of dust on the pavements. The neatly stacked houses that formed a solid wall either side of the cobbled streets seemed perfectly intact. Windowsills still held flowers and plants, gates were left half open as though the occupants had just gone through them, and the market stalls were still set up, though the produce in them was shrivelled and decayed. He waved his hand again, and the stalls cleaned themselves, the debris simply vanishing.

He slowly made his way down to the arena where the younglings were often found playing. It was next to the cliffs and, of course, the magix ring. There had been an older ring in the arena, but nobody had ever seen it working. It was thought that the new magix ring had rendered the earlier one useless, so it was nothing more than a relic. Then there was the Kalix ring, which worked but the platform it was on prevented others from stepping onto it. Shielding came up all round the platform to keep beings safe, while reading much more powerful levels of magix.

He suspected that both Lilah and Peter could stand in this one. If the older ring worked, could they be read by that one as well? A clear river ran the length of the entire continent and wound lazily through the mountains. Although, when he thought about it, around the time that his daughter had gone missing, a giant earthquake had shifted the entire landscape. The river still owed as it always had, yet the mountain near this part of it had seemingly moved. He remembered vividly that the ground had trembled in a way they'd never felt before, and then a cracking rent the air around them. They assumed at the time this was to do with Lilah's disappearance, and so they'd focused their searches here in the beginning. He sighed, his heart was racing.

This place held so many memories, and he wished more than ever he could talk to his love. Amanda. She'd always been the one who could calm him when he felt out of control. Now, standing here, he felt the loss stronger than he had in many years. Perhaps it was that he simply hadn't had time to mourn her yet, or because more than ever he wanted her to know that their Lilah was safe and well. She was so grown up and so immensely powerful, yet she'd nearly died because he'd wanted her to t in. It ate at him, the thought that his invention, the one meant to help her, had almost cost them her life.

How did anyone make amends for that? He didn't blame Damon for not wanting to be a part of his life now; he wouldn't either if he had the choice. His heart hurt so much, he wondered how it didn't just thump right out of his chest and fall to the ground in front of him.

As all these thoughts overwhelmed him, he picked fresh squash and broccoli. The tomatoes were upstream a little, and he worked his way up there, emptying his baskets magically as they filled, sending the goods straight to the kitchens. He laughed to himself, knowing he could've used magix to get the food supplies, but he needed the manual labour of picking them. He gathered all kinds of fruits and vegetables, and even mushrooms, which none of them had realised was a food source until they

Escape

were on Earth. He smiled, thinking of how much he'd learned in his time there. Amanda would've loved Earth. She craved new cultural experiences, and they had more than any other world.

Out the corner of his eye, Matthew caught a glimpse of something moving and turned to see it better. His heart sank when he realised it was his cottage, and the movement was Lilah's tree. It swirled and swayed, though there was no breeze strong enough to cause it. The berries shone brightly, large and plump, glistening in the sunshine. *Huh*. If her tree was still here, where had the other one come from? He'd thought Peter had called it to her using magix, but now it seemed that wasn't the case. Had he magixed it himself? If he had then had he also magixed the original one? If he did then it meant that Peter had powers as strong as the Creators. Was it possible? The Creators were the most ancient of magix beings. They had been all over the universe and were true immortals, Earth had records of some of them, fighting over their planet.

He'd been told of them by Peter and Lilah, but did they realise how much danger there would've been if the stories were true? Creators were not kind by nature, and they loved to destroy as much as they created. It meant nothing to them if their creations were sentient, as long as they got what they wanted. There were a few exceptions, of course, but it would be safe to assume they could've obliterated Earth by accident and not cared.

He decided to stop in at his cottage, just to see it again. As he neared the garden gate, he saw the flowers Amanda had planted right before she'd left for Helios, just two days before it was eradicated. They were stunning, of course; she'd been talented and known what to plant and where. He just gawked at the pretty multicoloured flowers blooming and crawling up the side of the cottage wall. It was as though there was a woven blanket keeping it cosy in the cool air. In the corner on the right side were Damon's toys. He'd loved to play as his mother gardened. He hadn't moved them; the attack had happened so fast, and he had been moved to a secure location. Then within days, the Huntowra had started attacking their world as well, and they'd been forced to leave. It had been a brutal attack. Many of his people had died trying to evacuate the villagers. Matthew had insisted on helping. As a royal, he was duty bound to his subjects, and he took that seriously.

It had been a week before he learned that all the Aggaron had been killed, including his loved ones. Evaliah had seen his son after the initial attack, but the woman who had him had died—they'd been found by the Huntowra while trying to get to Earth. He'd been heartbroken, and for years it had haunted him. Now, he marvelled at the second chance he'd somehow received. His son had made it to safety, and somehow, miraculously, so had his daughter. They'd even found each other, with no memories. That was fate. He'd never believed in it before, yet here was proof it existed. Nobody would dissuade him from that belief, and he would never take his children for granted again.

The interior of his cottage stood exactly as it had on the morning he'd last been here. Amanda had left a shawl on the back of the kitchen chair. He gathered it up and pressed it to his face. Tears fell fast and hot. How he missed her! The cloth smelled so strongly of her... He'd forgotten the calming effect it had on him, and he fell to his knees as grief rocked him. He spasmed as wave after wave of pain washed through him. He had no idea how long he knelt there in his kitchen crying and

Escape

clinging to the shawl, but when he stood again, his knees felt as though they'd fused in the bent position.

The sun was getting lower outside, and he moved quickly now to look in on the rest of his home. The last room he went into was the bedroom. He knew this would get him crying again, and he sucked in a ragged breath before shoving the door open. Tears sprang up immediately, and he swallowed hard before forcing himself to enter.

If anyone happened across him in this state, he would look like a scruffy, underfed, and possibly sickly person. His hair stuck out in weird places, and he needed a shave. But he didn't care. He was here to finally feel the pain he'd been suppressing all these years. He had a war to win, and grief would only hinder his efforts. Dealing with it now was better than freezing up in the battle eld. He made his way round his bedroom, touching objects as he went. It helped him feel more connected to his home, and his grief. Finally, he settled on his wife's side of their bed and sat gingerly, not wanting to disturb the last indentation she'd made. Her nightdress lay across her pillow as it always had. It was a tiny thing, but for some reason it overwhelmed him. Her wardrobe door stood ajar, with clothes draped over it as though she'd tried them on then changed her mind about wearing them yet hadn't tidied them up. He smiled. She'd always been in such a hurry.

Before he knew it, he was laughing and crying all at once. What a weird thing to do. Was he broken? He didn't really care if he was. Despite the agony, he was happy to be here. He'd needed this. After sitting there staring off into space for a long time, he finally got the courage to head back to the castle. He was about to leave the room when he spied Amanda's flower basket from the corner of his eye. She had taken this with her.

Why was it here? He went to it gingerly and picked it up. Before he had the chance to look in it, worried voices called out to him, and he rushed out to let them know he was ne with the basket still in his arms.

The men from the previous night were running about, shouting, and he waved and yelled loudly to get their attention.

"Hey, hey, it's all right. I'm over here. Sorry. I stopped in at my old home. Guess the time got away from me." He reddened.

"Shit, old man, we thought you were dead in a ditch or summik."

"Do you know we have been looking for you since lunchtime? Bosses said we gotta stay with ya from now on or we'll be shot."

"Yeah, and that ain't fair on us, see?"

He hadn't meant to cause so much worry. "I am so sorry. I needed to spend the day here. This was the last place my wife and I were together before she was murdered by the Huntowra. I feel really silly. My intention was to come right back and cook a nice lunch for us all." He shrugged, hoping the men would understand and not be too mad at him.

The one called Flanagan seemed to de ate. His eyes softened, and he nodded, clearly understanding. The other one huffed and turned away, stalking off in the direction of the castle. As they walked back, Matt was quiet, ashamed for today. Not for his emotions, just that it had scared the others and caused them to look for him when they had other duties. He promised himself right then that he wouldn't allow his grief to affect others in this war again. Flanagan was right; it wasn't fair on them. He

Escape

kept his eyes on the path, watching the other man disappear in the fading light.

"Sorry bout ya missus," Flanagan said softly.

Matt just nodded solemnly, not knowing what to say, but he didn't need to speak, because the other man went on.

"Lost me wife and unborn kid in a freak accident. There aren't many words to say for it, but I know how it is, needing to go back to the last place you was happy and wishing it was a bad dream instead of real, ya know?" He was barely audible. He shrugged, wiping his eyes on his forearms nonchalantly and avoiding Matt's gaze.

Matt was floored. He wanted to ask about the man's loved ones but didn't want to be rude. This was one of those times where he was unsure of human customs, so he strained to think of ways the people of Earth helped when someone lost their loved ones. Camping? No, that wouldn't help. Flowers? Flanagan didn't seem the sort to want those, and definitely not from a strange man. Then he remembered…

"We should have a drink to, you know, honour their memories," he said warily, not wanting to offend the other man.

Flanagan beamed. "Count me in," he said loudly and thumped Matt hard on the back.

He nearly buckled, but thankfully the other man didn't notice. They were back in the castle grounds now and talk shifted from death and grief. Flannagan had questions, lots and lots of them. From wanting to know about palace life to how Matt had become an inventor. Then he shared that in his everyday life, Flanagan was an artist. Not the painting type; he preferred glass blowing and resin pouring. Matthew hadn't heard of those things before and asked many questions of his own, mostly so they didn't have to talk about the palace yet again. But he discovered that he really was interested in the work the other man did for fun. It seemed Flanagan enjoyed the challenge and offered to show Matt how it all worked, if they ever got the chance.

With that, they caught up to the other man, who'd left them in the village. He was looking at them gloomily then stuffed a raw carrot in his mouth, clearly annoyed. Matt blinked. Why was the man so grouchy?

But then Flanagan roared with laughter and smacked his own forehead. "Aww, shit. You hangry, ey." He grinned at the other man, who glared back for a second before speaking.

"Yup. Been waiting all damn day for food that's real and not the crap we get from boxes, and then no one shows up to cook it, even after promising they would." He looked at Matt pointedly.

Oh. With a red face again, Matt set to work, and the other two talked while he made them dinner. He made a casserole, and added mashed potato, which he'd learned to make only recently. He wished he had potatoes here, but he had to make do with the packet potato provided with their ration packs. Then it occurred to him that there was no reason not to grow potato here. With that thought, he ate with more gusto then left Flanagan and the other man, saying goodnight on his way.

He bathed quickly, not wanting to linger in the tub. Then he went to his father's old study, the one he used for private moments, not his formal one. As he entered, he smelled wood ash, and sap. His father's cologne still clung to the air, and a sharp pain shot into Matthew's chest and up his left side. He

Escape

clutched at it, the pain increasing with each second. Bile rose up his throat. As he wiped his face, he realised he had a cold sweat and knew he needed help, right now. There were no healers here tonight, but Flanagan and the other man Miles could call for one. He teleported to them, and wordlessly collapsed.

"Shit, Matt! Flanagan, get the damn medical kit, *now*."

Miles was at his side in a flash, assessing his vitals. "Do you have pain?"

Matt nodded and pointed to his chest, his heartbeat racing like he'd run a marathon.

"Any other symptoms? Feel sick? Heartburn? Dizziness?"

Matt nodded as Miles listed symptoms. He had no idea what was going on, and he started to feel really tired. His eyes rolled.

"Get the Nitro-glycerin spray. He's having a heart attack," Miles shouted at Flanagan, and the other man threw a bottle to him. "Matt, I know you're tired right now, but I'm gonna give you some medicine to stop the heart attack. It's a spray, goes under your tongue. Doesn't taste too nice but it helps. We need to get some help as well. This is a patch, not a x. Ready? Here we are then." He pumped the spray under Matt's tongue.

He was right, it wasn't nice, but he was in no position to say anything about it.

"Ima call for the healers. Stay with him, 'kay?" Flanagan was all business for a change.

Matt felt a small amount of relief, and over the next half hour, he had two more doses of the spray before the healer made it to Meakra. Miles and Flanagan got a light blanket and pillow, trying to make him comfortable. He appreciated their kindness. He tried to sit up and was promptly pushed back down by Miles.

"Aw, hell naw. You need to stay there. Can't have a great cook like you up and dying on us now. Hey, boss?" He winked at Matt.

Matt blinked but was too unwell to really care that he was being bossed around.

* * *

Evaliah arrived on Meakra as quickly as she could, hoping she was in time to help. A message had been screamed out in the hallway of A.S.U, a man yelling that the emperor had suffered a heart attack and needed urgent help. She'd rushed to the meeting room, and a portal had already been opened. She strode through the palace quickly and was in the citadel within half an hour. Not her nest time, but she was here. She entered the informal lounge suite where she was told to go. Eva was about to close the door behind her then saw Matthew on the ground, propped up by Miles with Flanagan hovering over them, pacing and muttering.

She forgot all about the door and sucked in a sharp breath, the sound alerting both men to her presence. They ushered her forwards, and she almost tripped on a scatter cushion. She placed a hand on his forehead, cold beads of sweat scattering as she did. His breathing was shallow, and he wasn't conscious. She worked as fast as she could to restore his heart's rhythm then went to work on the other symptoms.

It was a long night. Evaliah stayed at Matthew's side, treating his new symptoms as they came up, and by morning, she was con dent he would survive. It was largely thanks to the quick thinking of the men and the spray they'd used to treat the

Escape

immediate episode. She'd learned much from her new friends on Earth, but this was one she hadn't yet seen in action. She was impressed. As she made her way down for breakfast, she bumped into Flanagan and stopped to say good morning. "How are you?"

"Ah, hey. How's the boss man doin?" He was wringing his hands, clearly worried for Matt's health.

She gave him a warm smile, reaching out and resting her dainty hand on his thick forearm. "He will recover fully. That spray medicine you used saved his life. I'm very impressed. Have you thought about being a healer...oh, I mean a nurse, or doctor maybe?" She was confused by the distinction between the two. In her experience, healers did the work of both doctor and nurse. There were things she just wouldn't get, ever, about humans.

"No, ma'am. I don't have the smarts for that. Gotta be good at maths and stuff." He blushed as they walked down the hall together. "But Miles was a paramedic. He's smart like that. But after...well, after stuff happened, he quit. Now he works here, but he still knows all the medical stuff, even though he's a cranky pants lots of the time."

Evaliah listened intently, and then an idea struck her, but she wouldn't say anything here. She would wait and present her idea when the time was right. She smiled serenely to herself.

* * *

By noon the next day, Matthew was up and starting to move about, though he was restricted by Miles, who, under Evaliah's instruction, was ensuring he wasn't overdoing it. Miles seemed rather fond of the healer. He certainly listened to each of her instructions intently and followed them to the tee. What was it about her that had won him over so quickly? Matt was still getting grumpy faces and one-word answers, barked grudgingly. He'd have to ask Eva how to win him over. He was grateful to the gruff man; he had saved his life, after all.

Every time he tried to talk to him on the first day, the other man seemed rather busy. Either he was urgently fixing something, talking to the others about 'stuff' or listening to his headphones. After trying all day to get his attention, Matt gave up, deciding to speak to Eva before trying again.

* * *

The base was fully operational now. After hearing what had happened, Bryant had taken the lead, moving the important council members into their designated areas and arranging for the soldiers to bunk at the training grounds, right next to the palace. The citizens of Meakra were scheduled to move home over the next three weeks, in batches. It had become obvious that they wanted to be in their own homes, and after negotiation, an agreement was reached. If the new wards held up, they could move back to their homes, but to start with they would all be in the east wing of the castle. It was only a small step forward, but it was possibly the most important one.

Matt sighed; he wanted to be back in his own cottage as well. He understood better than anyone what it was like to be so close yet so far from the place all his happiness had been. With the new wards up and the magix protection spells they'd created in the years since being forced out of their homes, he was sure this land was safe from the Huntowra. For now, at least. And yet, the Aggaron had believed that before they were attacked. He felt lost, not wanting to admit out loud how frightened he was, or how frail he felt. Most of the day was spent sitting and being fussed over.

Escape

But he attended meetings with Miles's help, though it felt awkward to have the younger man guide him with strong hands. It wasn't too long before his patience wore thin, and his temper started flaring, but when he lashed out, he was given a sedative and placed right next to a whole wall of Starling Trumpets. *Ha-ha. Very funny*, he thought to himself darkly. He knew it was for the best; after all, as soon as he began to get cranky, he also started feeling the pain in his chest again. After some lunch, he felt too exhausted to continue.

"Enough. I can't keep doing this today. Can we please reschedule the rest of the meetings for tomorrow?" He looked at Miles sadly, hating that he needed to ask.

Miles grimaced and nodded then helped Matt to his room. "Is there anything else I can get you?"

"Thank you, but no. I feel so silly needing this much help, actually."

"That's no reason to feel silly, boss. I was really worried about you yesterday, you know." He looked embarrassed to admit it.

Matt blinked. It hadn't occurred to him the other man was worried. Was that why he was so harsh? "Well, I would've panicked and might have had to watch you die if the roles were reversed. I'm afraid I'm not good with that kind of situation. I'd try, of course, but if there's no obvious wound, I sometimes don't see the person needs help until it's too late. It's a aw. Give me a war, and I can fight, but sickness…that's a whole different story."

"Most don't know what to do in a case like that. I was a paramedic back home before all this. I saw the subtle signs earlier and went looking after you didn't come back like you said. Then when we found ya, I stomped off, knowing that Flanagan would drag you right back to the palace. I pretended I was mad so you'd stay in sight, and I could monitor you. I didn't say anything cause I didn't wanna scare you, especially since that woulda been more stressful on the old ticker." He winked at Matt.

"There were subtle signs of this?"

"Yeah, there sometimes is. I've been noticing stuff over the last month or so. Told me other bosses, and they said to keep a watch on ya. You seemed to get paler, your left shoulder kept pulling down a bit, like it was hurting, and you'd grab at it or try to stretch it out. And since we came here, you got more tired than I ever saw you in all the time I've known ya. The day we got here, you were short of breath like you'd run a tonne, and you been eating heartburn medication like they're lollies. These are all signs of a heart attack. Then the other night when you couldn't breathe or speak and then collapsed…well, it made sense, didn't it?" He shrugged like this was the most common thing. Did he understand it wasn't?

"Well, actually, I didn't know you knew me that well, Miles. I thought you were new here, but I wanted to say thanks. I mean, for saving my life. I really am happy to be here today, even if it does annoy me not being able to just get back to work. I wanted to say it yesterday, actually, but things got in the way."

"Aww. Yeah, it's all good, boss. Just doin me job, hey. Listen, I'ma go help miss Eva. She said something 'bout setting up the infirmary wing." He shrugged but there was a smile there. "You stay here and get lots a rest. I mean it. Will tie ya down if I have to," he added sternly then left.

Escape

With nothing else to do, Matt simply sat in his overstuffed armchair and read a book. Not long after that, he fell asleep.

Chapter 17

LILAH'S TEAM

Lilah and her team were training hard. It had started slower than she would've liked but now they were in the groove of it, they didn't stop. Within a week, they'd progressed from learning basics to learning attack moves. A couple of weeks after that, they were working with teams from Halla, going out into the Qualterra and training against the Shrogan in the deepest ravines. There had been a few injuries to heal, of course, but not as many as Lilah had anticipated, and definitely not as serious as they could've been.

When they finished training with weapons, everyone pitched in to help Lilah and Amara with magix training. It was going better than expected. Amara had a natural are with magix, and she was more powerful than most who were born with it. Lilah's own magix was almost back to full strength. She hid most from the others for now, just to be sure no other being could sense her magix yet. Training started when the sun rose, and they often had to be halted for meals. All the teams were committed, seemingly using each other to compete for who could endure the most. And all of them stayed after the sun set, fighting under the stars, which were incredible on Qualterra. The night sky showed planets and rings that weren't visible in the day. You could nearly reach up and touch them they were so close. Tonight was no different; they were all there again, training and trying out new ideas.

Escape

Hannah loved looking at the stars, but there wasn't time to do that here. She had to stay focused. Lilah was coming again. Her arm swayed as it did right before an attack, and instinctively she shielded herself. The timing was perfect. She hadn't been able to do it until now, always self-conscious. The others all thought of her as a healer and not a fighter, but fighting was as much in her blood as the healing ability was. Her father was a Talgra, after all. She'd been surprised when Lilah and Emma cornered her, asking her to come train with them. It had really frightened her, but it was the best way to be helpful. Her skin practically zinged with anticipation of the coming war. She, like all Visper, was very sensitive to conflict. It had a physical effect on them.

She twirled as Lilah passed her, having missed her mark before. As she turned to counter, a great *thwack* sounded from nearby. Both the women stopped and looked round curiously. There was a small group of Shrogan near, though they couldn't be detected by them at the moment.

"That's odd. They generally stay on the other side of the ravine," Emma mused, walking over slowly and watching the gathering cautiously.

"Yeah, wonder what's riled them," Caleb added. He and Emma had formed a bond in the last few weeks, which made Hannah and Lilah smile, just a little.

"Well, whatever happened, maybe we should head home anyway. As beautiful as this place is in the dark…or semi dark, we need to rest and eat. Dale's gone and cooked again. It's that stew stuff you love so much, Cal." Emma swung to face him and crossed her arms, knowing what his reaction would be then smirked when he jumped in the air, fist pumping and whooping for joy. She laughed then set to work opening a portal.

"So, first I shielded then I twisted back but it wasn't quite right and—" Hannah began.

"Shut up already, would ya? Sheesh, don't you ever stop talking…like *ever?*" Caleb teased.

Hannah just rolled her eyes at him and continued, though she was quieter.

* * *

Dale and Lilah were listening intently, glancing at each other every now and then. They had a language of their own. Both grinned when Dale nearly choked on some bread Caleb had made. It was delicious, more rustic than his own breads. The texture reminded him of something, but he couldn't place it.

"Well, it's past bedtime. Way past it, actually. Sleep well. Tomorrow, I'll be training with you as well." He clapped his hands together and dropped a kiss on his daughter's hair then excused himself for the night.

Happiness filled his heart despite the circumstances that had brought them together. He'd opened his home to all his daughter's friends; they found places on couches and floors to sleep.

He hummed the little melody he'd always known as he went about getting ready for bed, preferring to do it without magix. His night trousers were soft and warm, with laces in the waist to tighten or loosen as needed. They were a plain cream colour; he never cared for patterned materials, and only wanted his garments to be comfortable and practical. He went to his small wash basin and cleaned his face then combed his hair.

Looking into the mirror, he wondered again if he would ever get his memories back. He tried not to think of it too often,

Escape

it always made him sad, but there were times when he just couldn't escape the thoughts. He smelled something sweet in the air, as he'd done in the past. There was no cause for the sweet smell, and his heart hurt when it hit him. Tears sprang up for no reason he could tell, so he blinked rapidly to get rid of them then climbed into bed, gruffly pulling the blankets round him. He fell asleep right away and woke feeling like he hadn't slept at all.

His poor sleep showed as he made his morning meal, tidied the kitchen, and dressed for the day. He was lacing his boots when he heard the others. The sound was sudden, and it startled him. Not easy to do. He had surprisingly fast reflexes and wasn't scared by much. He put it down to poor sleep. He smacked his cheeks as he straightened, gave his head a shake, and went to retrieve his sword from the hall where he kept it.

A loud rumbling started as he secured the fastenings, and he looked round, bracing against the wall. Dust stirred from the rafters and showered him, falling like rain and pooling on his shoulders. He was frozen to the spot. He'd done this before, but not here. Somewhere else. Another time he'd been anxious and hadn't slept well, sounds had woken him and he'd sprung into action. The images flashed fast, and he didn't even have time to process them before they faded again. It took him a few minutes to gather himself.

***

Lilah looked up as Dale made his way into the room. Something had happened. She was about to ask what when there was a loud knocking from the front of the house. Dale opened the door, and there was Mierden in human form, rocking on his heels with a grin of excitement, and Mirren standing near the gate looking morosely at some bees hovering over the bowers overgrowing in the front garden.

"Well, that was a wonderful start to the day, wasn't it?" Mierden clapped loudly, clearly happy about the tremor.

"Erm, no, not really. Actually, it kind of sucked," Caleb answered, despite not being asked anything. He had a handful of bread and a bowl, and shoved food into his mouth as he stood behind Dale, as though the other man wasn't even there.

Dale fought back a grin, and simply raised his eyebrows in answer to Mierden's apparent disgust for the obnoxious man.

"Well, let's get on with it then." He turned and walked up the road with his son flouncing along behind him.

"What's up his arse?" Caleb snorted.

"Not everyone appreciates your opinion, Cal," Emma supplied acidly. She shoved past him and headed off in the same direction as the others.

"Meh meh meh meh," Caleb intoned, mocking Emma. He stepped forward at the same time Hannah did and fell with a loud *thud* onto the stone path, mumbling into the dirt as Hannah apologised loudly and picked herself up. She didn't bother checking if he was okay; she just ran off to catch up with Emma.

Dale roared with laughter and Lilah simply stood near Caleb without saying a word. Amara said her farewells. She was heading into the next village for advanced magix training with the elders today. She smiled at Caleb as she stepped over him and laughed softly as the gate swung shut behind her.

"You knew that was gonna happen, didn't ya?" he accused Lilah.

"No idea what you mean, Cal. Come on or we'll be late." She turned away, but not before Dale saw her wink and give a hint of a smile.

Escape

Yep, she'd known all right. He walked slower than the others and thought about the little team she'd brought here. Though they were so different and clearly some were more advanced than others, they all seemed to blend well together. They teased each other, they fought among themselves, but they also trusted each other deeply. He'd seen it several times since they arrived. Cal was the lesser of them all in his mind, yet the others put up with his rudeness and lack of power. Why? Maybe today he would get to see why they all allowed him to be a part of this team, because to him the man made no strategic sense at all.

He caught up with them as the portal opened into Qualterra, and he silently followed them through. He was assessing them today; it would be a long day for them all.

Dale shifted into his warrior patterns and began the training without any warning. They should've been prepared for anything; they had been warned and he wasn't going to be easy on them because they knew him. He swung out. His sword edges had been shielded so he didn't hurt anyone, but he needn't have worried. He was met with lightning-fast re exes and a swift counter. Cal seemed to feel the change in atmosphere and reacted without any hesitation. He spun, a sword he'd borrowed already up and shielding his face. And before anyone could blink, he had shifted from shielding to attacking, letting his whole body do the work for him. He spun in a circle, his feet gliding effortlessly while he moved his sword as though it were an extension of himself and let it collide with Dale's sword as he fluidly shifted.

* * *

A smirk appeared on the other man's face, and they began to trade blows. Dale had strength and experience, but Cal had his instinct, and he let himself relax into the battle. He had learned young that tensing in battle made you rigid and *that* could become a weakness. Of course, being relaxed was as well, but it worked better for him, so he went with it. It also prevented him from getting confused and disoriented, which was a bonus. Cal laughed as time went on, holding his own. The two men battled for an hour before the others called for them to stop.

"Why? Come on, Em, we were just starting to have fun."

"Look over in the distance, you dolt."

"What the fuck?" As he looked, several large shapes headed toward them, their wings causing dust to fly up from the ground.

It took a moment for him to realise that they were dragons, and he stared open-mouthed as they performed complicated moves, twisting and diving in all directions at different heights. After a few minutes of this sky dance, a large, rusty-looking dragon missed a beat and fell with a loud thud that they all felt. He roared, clearly angry, and shook himself out.

After a few minutes, everyone got back into training, switching out with each other as the day went on. The dragons stayed close, and by late afternoon, everyone was tired and hungry. They stopped for a short break, chewing on protein bars that Caleb had thoughtfully packed.

"Mm, these aren't so bad. Reminds me of lizard and nuts," the rusty dragon commented sarcastically.

"Osmases, be more thankful. It was a gift of kindness. He did not have to give you that to fill your belly," another dragon chided him.

Escape

"Naw, it's okay. I think it's funny, actually." Caleb grinned enthusiastically at them. "They taste horrible, but they're loaded with goodness. We have them because sometimes there's no re, or stove, or food sources. This is just a way to stay alive and healthy. Well, healthier than if we had nothing at all." He shrugged.

The dragons considered him thoughtfully. He didn't know what they were thinking, and it didn't matter to him anyway. He was the odd guy out here, and he worried that Lilah had made a mistake when she said he was meant to be a part of this team. Regardless, he was here now and determined to be useful. Often, he passed off his insecurities as boisterousness or by acting foolish, but he was neither usually. He just rubbed people the wrong way sometimes, so he'd decided to use it as a mask. It kept anyone from asking him too many questions he wasn't willing to answer. His bosses knew everything, and that was all that mattered to him.

The other advantage was that it threw people off. He seemed so casual and cavalier, yet he was constantly alert and watched everything. Even Dale had taken his attitude for complacency and attacked him first. In truth, he'd known it was coming. He'd taken Dale's warning seriously so had been ready to battle even with his back turned. He'd seen Dale's tell as he'd entered the portal, his hand shifting unconsciously toward his sheath, his thumb hooking into the button to open it. Everyone had a tell, and he saw it within seconds. It was something he'd learned from a young age, to survive.

He thought now about Osmases and how he'd collided with the ground. His left wing had curled downwards slightly— a tell there was weakness in that wing. He didn't think the others had seen it, so he would find a time to tell the dragon without being overheard. If he, a lowly human, could see it then surely the enemy would too and use it to their advantage.

"The air's becoming static. We should seek shelter if we're staying here the night. There will be a storm soon," Mierden spoke quietly but with conviction.

Talk erupted all round, some wanting to leave and come back, but others saying they should stay. Cal didn't know if he wanted to stay or not, but he didn't think there should be a choice, really.

"We wouldn't get to go home during a war on Earth, so why here? Seems to me we should stop sulking. This is war, no matter how quiet it feels now. We won't get to exit the battle eld once the Huntowra attack. I figure the best we can do is learn safe places to shelter." He hadn't meant to say it out loud, but nobody seemed to think it was wrong.

"He's right. Besides, I want to check out the cave network we heard about," Mirren stated quietly, and his father shot him a look that was hard to explain. Was the older dragon angry with his son? Mirren stared straight back at the older man but didn't say more.

The caves that had wider openings weren't safe for shelter —they were frequented by Shrogan and easily targeted by the Huntowra—so the group headed for the smaller caves instead. Many of them were nothing more than shallow holes, useful to go into in an emergency but not the safest places. They started to map the ones that could be used for weapons caches or for the healers to be stationed in case they were needed in the battle eld. Having non-combatants in the ring line didn't sit well with anyone from Earth, but every other species of being said it

Escape

was normal for them to be near to heal wounded warriors quickly.

They found smaller caves that went downwards, winding narrow passageways that were so tight in some places you had to turn sideways and squeeze through. They checked several of these as the afternoon wore on. It was worth the effort, as they found a few where several other tunnels connected to the main one, all looping back on themselves and continuing further in. After a while, the narrow paths widened then opened into a spectacular underground cavern.

Enormous crystal-like structures filled the massive space, and small holes from above shot light onto several of the crystals, which scattered the light in all directions. A large underground lake sat off to their left, the banks stretching as far as they could see. The ground crunched under their shoes. Shells, sand, and rocks littered the ground, and cactus-looking plants grew like an underground forest. Bordering the walls in places, tall trees grew. There was an entire ecosystem here. It was an overwhelming sight, though Lilah wasn't surprised by it.

"Wow," someone whispered.

"You got that right," Cal replied, just as softly. "This place...it's huge. Did anyone else know this was here?" Dale asked, staring around in wonder. He wandered towards the lake's edge and jumped when something moved in the water. "Argh, what was that?"

"Scared of a little shy, are we?" Cal snorted.

Dale ushed and snapped his mouth shut. He wanted to smack the smugness off the younger man's face, but this wasn't the time or place for personal drama. They had bigger things to worry about, and this cavern would solve a lot of their problems.

P Ryall

They explored the area for a while then settled into a protected area between the forest of cactus and the water. They set up their tents and scavenged for redwood.

When they'd made a re, they sat round it, discussing the possibilities. It seemed that none of the Shrogan frequented these caverns, so they didn't have to worry about that. Some of the larger caves could be accessed by the Huntowra, but it was possible to have armed personnel guarding the entrances. This place had drinkable water, there were clearly fish of some kind here, it was sheltered from bad weather and Shrogan attacks, and it was lit well— though light was never a problem with all the magix beings.

They learned that there were also other small creatures here, ones that were edible. To the humans, they looked like rabbits. The dragons called them rodents, and Dale knew of them as Star-spirits. They were called this in many cultures because the meat gave you a mild high when you ate it. Seers used the meat of Star-spirits to communicate with the energy of the universe; it helped heighten their abilities.

Lilah watched her friends, but her mind was also seeing other things. It came on suddenly, and she knew that this was the day it all changed. She needed to alert everyone— her mother and brother on Earth, her father on Meakra, and of course, Peter and the others on Helios. They would pass the message onto all the others, but right now, she had to tell her team. Dale and Cal started bickering again. Mierden and Mirren were also having a heated disagreement, though she didn't know what it was about. Osmases and another dragon were wrestling, and Emma was practicing sword fighting with Hannah, who was a natural with a blade, though she preferred axes over swords.

Escape

Just as she was about to yell for their attention, she felt massive energy that could only mean one thing. The Huntowra were here, large numbers of them. It was only a few seconds before everything around her suddenly stopped, with the exception of the humans. They all stared around in horror, knowing this could only mean one thing. Dale looked at his daughter, and she sadly smiled. Yes, it was time. She let her magix ow and opened a connection to all the magix rings she could feel. As each ring activated, she projected herself standing there, and spoke to all who were nearby.

"It has begun. The Huntowra army are gathering in the Qualterra and are about to attack. Get ready. It's time." She disconnected from the rings and looked around her. She had no more words for them. This was exactly how it had to be. The Huntowra were here, but they didn't know anyone else was. They believed they had the element of surprise. The Huntowra were hiding in large numbers on several worlds that had been unwatched by others, which was why Lilah had suggested to her father and their allies that having outposts on several worlds was a good idea. It had been a subtle manipulation, in order to ensure that as many of them survived as possible. Not everyone would, though. The pain of her many gifts was knowing that no matter what she did, others would still suffer. She saw pieces of paths as they laid out each moment, every choice made by the Huntowra making the path clearer, and she adjusted accordingly. But this wasn't a game in her head; she was condemning some to death so others could live.

She glanced at Dale, wanting so much more time to just be near him. He made her feel whole, and safe. He looked pale, more so in the cavern's light. Cal stood near him, and though neither man spoke nor touched in any way, she knew they were comforting each other in this moment. Dale's surety and Cal's hyper awareness both clashed and complemented each other. That was why she'd wanted the boisterous man to be part of this team: his skills were well-matched to Dale, and his acute reactive nature meant that he was one of only a few who could actually hold his own against him in a battle.

They would fight back-to-back, and their friendship would grow from there. Dale was about to have his first best friend. Someone he thought inferior now was destined to help him in his coming journey. She didn't see the path Dale was on other than this, but she knew it was important Cal was part of it.

ALSO BY P RYALL

THE MAGIX SERIES
AVAILABLE NOW

Refugees Escape

* * *

ALSO IN THE SERIES
COMING SOON

The Fall of the Aggaron (Prequel)

Huntowra

Creators

P Ryall

About the Author

www.ingramcontent.com/pod-product-compliance
Lightning Source LLC
Chambersburg PA
CBHW052027070526
44584CB00016B/1928